ACCIDENTAL COMPLIANCE PROFESSIONAL

LESSONS LEARNED FROM 23 YEARS IN THE INDUSTRY

ROY J. SNELL

SCCE™

PRAISE FOR *THE ACCIDENTAL COMPLIANCE PROFESSIONAL*

Margaret Hambleton, CHC, CHPC, President, Hambleton Compliance: *"A thoroughly enjoyable must-read, for every compliance professional. The book is a wonderful combination of all of Roy's best qualities: wisdom, passion, experience, humor, and just the right amount of wise cracker. I've known Roy for almost twenty years and still found I had more to learn from him."*

Alison Taylor, Managing Director at Business for Social Responsibility: *"Roy Snell's energy, curiosity, sense of adventure, and fun suffuses every paragraph of this book. Via personal anecdotes ranging from college pranks gone wrong to tackling integrity challenges in Sarajevo, makes a compelling case that compliance officers are the heart and conscience of the corporation, and that the mission has never been more important."*

Donna Boehme, "Lion of Compliance": *"Roy Snell is the storyteller the compliance profession needs and deserves! Every CCO needs the wisdom in this book! #ROWRR! #StandingOnTheShouldersOfGiants"*

Joe Murphy, Senior Analyst, Compliance Strategists: *"Go right to chapter 8. If you don't agree with this chapter, then don't read this book. In fact, don't go into compliance at all. Do something else completely. But if chapter 8 hits you, then read this book and become a compliance and ethics professional."*

Gerry Zack, CEO of HCCA/SCCE: *"No, Joe—I gotta disagree. It's all about chapter 12 on the dangers of rationalization! Roy really nails it in his discussion of this critical issue."*

Debbie Troklus, Senior Managing Director, Ankura: *"So many of us are accidental compliance officers and [Roy's] stories are both humorous and reflective of the journey."*

Haydee Olinger, former Global Chief Compliance Officer, McDonald's Corporation: *"Roy Snell has hit the nail on the head. His anecdotes and wisdom will inspire you to improve yourself and your organization."*

Garrett Reisman, former NASA astronaut and engineer and current Director of Space Operations at SpaceX: *"Lesson 2 really resonated with me since Roy's 'belt and suspenders' approach is very similar to the exhaustive contingency planning and redundancy that we rely upon to keep our human spaceflight missions as safe as possible."*

Bojan Bajić, CEO of Net Consulting, Ltd.: *"Roy Snell is the first to apply spiritual growth tips to the complexities of the compliance profession, making his book a practical guide to becoming both a happy and successful compliance and ethics professional."*

Odell Guyton, former Director of Compliance at Microsoft and cofounder of SCCE: *"The compliance profession as a whole owes a great deal to the accidental underpinnings of this compliance pioneer."*

Jay Jorgensen, Global Chief Ethics and Compliance Officer of Walmart: *"Roy may have become a compliance professional by accident, but he also became one of the profession's founding fathers. This account provides insight and direction for compliance professionals today."*

Jim Sheehan, Chief, Charities Bureau, New York Attorney General's Office: *"Compliance ideas and their emotional context come out through collecting used anvils from the Rust Belt, watching NASCAR crashes, wrecking his stepmother's Delta 88 as a teenager, and being yelled at for ten minutes in his first compliance job by a corporate bully while his junior colleague looked on."*

The Accidental Compliance Professional: Lessons Learned from 23 Years in the Industry
is published by the Society of Corporate Compliance and Ethics, Minneapolis, MN.

ISBN 978-1-7335986-0-6

Editor: Karen Latchana Kenney
Designer: Craig Micke

Society of Corporate Compliance and Ethics
6500 Barrie Road, Suite 250
Minneapolis, MN 55435
p +1 952 933 4977 or 888 277 4977 | f +1 952 988 0146
corporatecompliance.org | helpteam@corporatecompliance.org

This book is dedicated to my parents Marge and Jud Snell, who were flawed, honest, ethical, trusting, and respectful of others. When I wonder why I have found such a comfortable place in the compliance community, I always think of them. They gave me a strong foundation of humor and integrity, which has helped me in every aspect of my life.

My mother, who told it like it was and treated everyone with respect.

My father, who helped me take honesty and integrity seriously.

CONTENTS

ACKNOWLEDGEMENTS

I want to thank my greatest mentor Marc Dettmann, who taught me many of the lessons that you'll find in this book. I want to thank my family—Julie, Jessica, Abbie, Erin, and Anna—for helping me become a better person. Much credit for this book goes to Karen Latchana Kenney, who essentially cowrote it and made it so much better. There are way too many compliance mentors to thank, such as Dan Roach, Debbie Troklus, Sheryl Vacca, Margaret Hambleton, Odell Guyton, Joe Murphy, and Donna Boehme, to mention a few. Most of all I want to thank every compliance professional who has ever communicated with me. This book is essentially the result of all the wisdom you have given me. **RJS**

FOREWORD

I may know Roy Snell better than anyone, except his closest family members. We have worked closely together professionally for more than 20 years. We both share an obsession with rusty old tools and machines, which has meant hundreds of hours together at estate sales, swap meets, auctions, or old farms trying to score real or perceived treasures. Moreover, we both share a passion for the wilderness, which led to a personal partnership for the past 10 years—together we own a remote northern Ontario lake property 50 miles from the nearest pavement or power pole, 12 miles from the end of the road, and 18 miles from the nearest private property. On a good day it is a 12-hour trip to get to the place. We've talked about everything under the sun in the hundreds of hours we spend together each year, but more than anything else, we've talked about compliance.

I had the good fortune as a young lawyer to stumble into compliance in the early 1990s. After having spent a year helping defend against a significant government investigation, in 1993 I was handed the task of implementing the first compliance program ever imposed by the federal government on a healthcare provider. Ultimately, I participated nearly 50 times in the defense of my organization's DOJ, FBI, or OIG investigations. Not long after setting up the compliance program in Minnesota, I was recruited to California to set up the compliance program for one of the largest healthcare systems in the country. It was about that time that Roy called asking if I would consider joining the Health Care Compliance Association . . . he had me hooked in about three minutes.

Roy's passion for compliance is as real as it gets, and on a recent road trip from Minnesota to Kansas City the conversation quickly turned to Roy's favorite subject—compliance. I had discovered 10 anvils in Kansas City and asked if he wanted to join me for the nine-hour each way road-trip to pick them up, sweetening the pot with the offer of a chance for him to do his own treasure hunting. As usual, 15 minutes into the trip, Roy was already talking about compliance and (again) as usual I was captivated (perhaps occasionally captive) by his perspective on compliance— compliance failures, compliance officers, governance, and countless other topics. On virtually every trip with him, I learn a bit more about Roy, and this trip was no exception. I heard some familiar stories, but what really caught my attention were several new stories about how he became a resident assistant at Michigan State University (see Lesson 4). The stories only took 15 minutes, but we talked about the lessons those experiences taught him for hours. Roy is a great storyteller. More important, however, he is a master at using his and others' experiences to shape and refine his (and others') behavior. This mastery is on full display in the pages that follow.

In addition to being passionate about what he does, Roy is laser-focused on his goals. Many people spend their lives planning, but Roy has spent his life doing. He understood a long time ago that people should get paid for achievement, not just activity. He can adapt and change, and is willing to listen (albeit briefly, as listening often interferes with doing). As you will learn in the lessons that follow, Roy can be a remarkably patient person. He recognizes that neither Rome nor compliance programs are built in a day. And like Timex, he can take a licking and keep on ticking. However, if you want to see Roy's "hair on fire," it only takes one simple phrase: *let's form a committee*. It's not that Roy is uncomfortable with committees—he *despises* committees. He doesn't believe it adds value to talk about doing something; he wants to actually get something done. While he is adaptable enough to have worked with committees when the organizational culture required it, I feel fairly certain that no committee was ever created at his behest.

When conference registrations were lagging, the solution in many associations was to form a committee to talk about the economy, tight industry budgets, program content, or lack of supposed "headliners" to attract attendees. Roy's reaction was very different, however, and it was always the same thing: more marketing . . . more marketing . . . and just when you thought you could do no more marketing, he would ask for more marketing. Not surprisingly, when most associations were shrinking after the 2008 crash, SCCE and HCCA continued to rapidly grow. The HCCA had a conference scheduled in Washington, DC, a few weeks after 9/11. The decision to move forward with the event wasn't made by a committee; it was made by Roy in a two-minute phone call. Many of the lessons in this book reflect his bias for action.

While Roy has had some grand ideas, he's always been eminently practical at his core. Roy not only helped grow SCCE and HCCA, he helped shape the two organizations' memberships to ones dedicated to *sharing* information, rather than hoarding it. He didn't want conference speakers who talked about theory, he wanted conference sessions that focused on the practical. He wanted to send attendees home with information that went beyond the *why*, and was focused on the *what* and *how*. Roy didn't want to talk about ethics, he wanted to change culture and behavior. The lessons shared in this book will encourage and motivate, but most of all they will help you do the things that drive compliance.

I have been learning from and with Roy for 20 years, yet I learned some new things in this book. For those of you who have been at this for a long time, you might recognize some of the professional and life lessons that Roy shares. For those of you who are relatively new to this challenging (but very rewarding) profession, the lessons in this book contain practical wisdom packaged in an entertaining delivery that is genuinely Roy—a legendary pioneer and leader in the compliance fraternity, and a remarkable colleague and friend to me.

Dan Roach
January, 2019

INTRODUCTION
ONE SENTENCE
CHANGED EVERYTHING

It was probably around 1995, the midpoint of my career. I was managing close to 30 people who determined what doctors should charge for their services. CEO Marc Dettmann and I were walking down the hallway and he had a long document in his hand. It was written by someone in the enforcement community—probably a *few* someones. The document was a settlement between the enforcement community and a prominent organization. Of all the rambling pages of legalese, Marc had turned to one page and was pointing to *one sentence*.

"It says here that their organization has agreed to hire a compliance officer and implement a compliance program. Maybe we should do that before they come visit us?" he said. By "they," Marc meant the enforcement community. I nodded and told him that it sounded like a good idea, but I really didn't have a clue how brilliant his summary of this convoluted document was. He saw the enforcement train coming. Years later, this and several other insightful decisions Marc made saved our organization somewhere around $30 million.

"Why don't *you* be our compliance officer?" Marc asked me.

I was still operating at about 30 leagues under his sea. I did not have a clue as to what he was asking me to do . . . no clue what a compliance and ethics officer was or how a compliance and

THE GREATEST MENTOR: MARC DETTMANN

Roy J. Snell, Aaron Gray, Andy North, and Marc Dettmann at a golf outing, mid-1990s

In 1995, Marc Dettmann saw something very important that most of us could not see—the beginning of the compliance profession. This was not surprising, since Marc had a Harvard law degree and a Wharton MBA. More important to me, he was just a regular guy with mass quantities of common sense. And not just one kind of common sense; Marc had many different kinds of common sense. He dressed like a regular guy instead of a CEO, walked like a regular guy, and talked like a regular guy. Most people I had met before then only saw the forest for the trees. Marc could see through the forest, the trees, the leaves, and down to some microscopic organism of great importance to his organization. That day when he asked me to become a compliance officer, he had read through all the legal mumbo-jumbo and pulled out one sentence that would have a huge impact on his organization and ultimately, in my vivid imagination, on all industries and countries around the world. To Marc, it was just another day of trying to make sure he and his organization were successful. I owe a lot to Marc, the greatest mentor I would ever have.

ethics program functioned, but I was honored that he thought I could do more for him.

"I'd be glad to," I told him.

That's what I always said to anyone who ever asked me to do something new—"sure." I had no plan for my career, but "sure" opened doors. Little did I know at the time, but that answer would change my life forever.

CREATING HCCA AND SCCE

As a result of my accidental entry into compliance, my career would zig and then zag very randomly. I would learn a lot of different lessons, all of which I would eventually use when I finally got to create something. That "something" I and a couple other people created would become the largest professional associations for compliance and ethics professionals in the world—the Health Care Compliance Association (HCCA) and the Society of Corporate Compliance and Ethics (SCCE).

Here's how it all started. About a year into my first compliance role, an employee of mine gave me Mary Dunaway's business card and said I should call her—she was the corporate compliance officer for University Physician's, Inc. I didn't always listen to this somewhat difficult employee, but luckily I did this time and called Mary.

During our long conversation, I was particularly intrigued with Mary because I had never met another compliance officer. I can't tell you how strange it was to have a new job at the age of 40 that I'd never heard of before. On top of that, I'd never met another person with the same job as me. Clueless doesn't begin to describe my state of mind.

Now that we'd joined forces, I suggested to Mary that we hold a meeting in Minneapolis for compliance officers. We tacked it onto the Medical Group Management Association conference and then searched the internet for compliance officers to invite. We found a few, mostly those who had been hired after the government forced their companies to do so. As I recall, we invited 30 people . . . and 65 *showed up*. They came from across the country for what would be the first meeting designed for and run by compliance officers.

That day—October 13, 1996—was surreal. The room was full of people who spoke my language. Mary and I saw that there were more of us than we realized. During that three-and-a-half-hour meeting, we all learned so much about the role of a compliance officer and the function of a compliance program. At the end of the meeting, I got up, thanked everyone, and said, "We need to start a group." Then Brent Saunders, the Thomas Jefferson University compliance officer, came up to me and said, "I need to be involved." We went to dinner that night and started thinking about what kind of organization we could form. I wrote "Health Care Compliance Association" on one side of a napkin and then a short mission statement on the other side.

What I would give for that napkin now. Our mission was simple: we wanted HCCA to be "a collaborative forum promoting integrity and ethical behavior through the development of comprehensive compliance programs throughout the entire health care industry."[1]

I told Brent we needed Debbie Troklus; she seemed like someone who could help us start this new organization. I found her at the conference and she said, "Not interested. I am an interim compliance officer." Luckily, I got her to agree to help anyway . . . and she went on to create the most significant set of credentials for compliance professionals in the history of our profession.

We were doing something completely new—something none of us really knew how to do, but we quickly figured it all out. We invited people we knew to serve on the board and then each took a part of operations, because we had no staff. Debbie made up a one-page membership brochure, started getting checks, and called me asking, "What do I do with this money?" I told her, "Open up a bank account." Around 50 people became members that year, when we sent out our first newsletters,

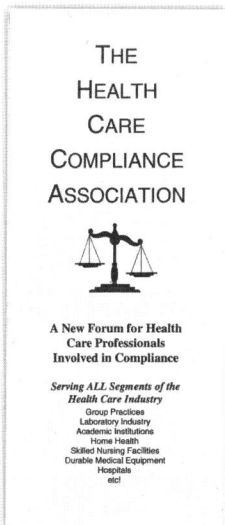

One of HCCA's first newsletters (left) and its first membership brochure (right)

From early on, I found that sitting in between sessions and talking with conference attendees was one of the best ways to understand what was going on in the compliance industry.

started a listserv, created a simple website, and organized our first educational programs as membership benefits.

Brent suggested I become the first president of HCCA . . . and I agreed. Our first real office space was a room with a desk, computer, and phone, donated to us by Marc at the organization where I was working as a compliance officer. We hired a temp as our first employee—Henry Youmans, who stayed with us for the next few years. And we held HCCA's first annual conference in Los Angeles in November 1997. We called it the National Health Care Fraud and Abuse Symposium. We had 24 speakers and 152 attendees.

After two years as president, I passed the baton to Brent: HCCA's second president. Things were growing so fast . . . it was a bit frightening, actually. By 2000, a few of our board members became concerned that the president's role was

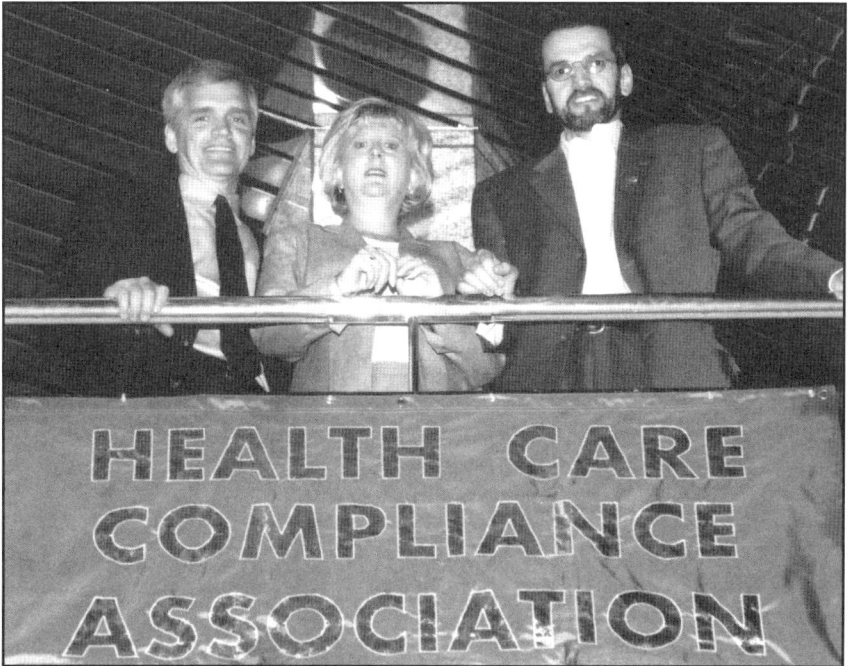

Greg Warner, Debbie Troklus, and Roy J. Snell, at one of HCCA's first annual conferences

consuming too much time, as the organization was getting bigger and more complicated. So, the board decided to hire a CEO. They sent the president at that time—Greg Warner, the compliance officer of the Mayo Clinic—to come see if I wanted the job. We worked everything out and I became CEO in February 2001. Just three years later, we started SCCE. As of early 2019, HCCA and SCCE hold more than 100 conferences each year all over the world. And the two associations now have more than 20,000 combined members. *Who knew?*

LESSONS FROM AN ACCIDENTAL COMPLIANCE PROFESSIONAL

From the compliance big bang and my accidental entry into the industry to now, I've learned countless compliance and ethics lessons. I've blindly started a couple of very significant things in my life. I'd reach some point in each journey that turned out to be supremely difficult and think I'd made a huge mistake. Those journeys are the ones I now treasure. The pain is long gone, but the benefits of those journeys will be at my side for the rest of my life.

We all learn differently. Sadly, I do not learn well from a book. I do not learn well from a lecture. I learn from doing— and making mistakes. Much of what I am going to share with you in this book are the lessons I have learned from my experiences and how they apply to running a compliance program.

ROY-ISMS

Throughout this book, you'll see "Roy-isms." They're phrases I say to describe something I believe to be true in a simplistic, yet interesting, way. *I tend to repeat them a lot.* Some may be considered funny (and I enjoy that response), but all have a serious underlying purpose or meaning.

These lessons are intended for future and current compliance and ethics professionals working in a compliance department that uses all seven elements of a compliance and ethics program. My hope is that on the days when you are immersed in the smoke, fire, and sparks of a big compliance issue, you will stop for a moment and remember an idea from this book. Then you'll do what is needed to be successful and find greater peace and success for yourself and your organization.

For those of you thinking about entering the compliance profession: *come on in, the water is warm.* It might be full of sharks, but it's still warm. If you are already a compliance and ethics professional, you may wonder: *how did I get into this*

LEARNING FROM THE STARS

This is my favorite picture ever taken at one of our conferences—people networking was what it was all about.

Many of my experiences have connected me with the stars of compliance—the early compliance professionals who became teachers and mentors. They fanned out into the compliance universe and gave presentations, wrote articles, published books, posted on blogs, shared thoughts on social media, did podcasts, and some even made short videos with tips of the day. The most valuable help provided by these stars of compliance happened in between sessions at conferences, when new compliance officers who needed a little help asked them questions very specific to their particular issues.

People outside of compliance have stopped by our conferences and occasionally remarked on their positive and collaborative atmosphere. Visitors to our profession have frequently remarked on how giving compliance professionals are. We've loved getting together at these conferences, because we went from an environment where few people understood us (our coworkers) into a room full of people who totally got us (our peers). I doubt any profession has such a remarkable gap between their professional colleagues' understanding of what their purpose is and their coworkers' understanding. That is one of the many challenges compliance professionals face, and it's why having a network of compliance stars is so important.

One of those stars is someone I continue to learn from. She's the first compliance professional to ever tell me I was wrong—Cathy Boerner, who I've known for 22 years. She was the first of many people to tell me I was wrong and she turned out to be right. I told Cathy a little about this book and the first suggestion she had was, "You better tell them about having emotional intelligence. In fact, you should make the whole book about emotional intelligence." Once again Cathy was right. Emotional intelligence is arguably the most important thing for a compliance professional to have. That's really what this book is all about: many ideas that I got from thousands of compliance professionals from what feels like millions of conversations. Everything I know was stolen from people like Cathy.

mess? If so, I am here to tell you that within the mess you'll find greatness all around you. You'll learn things you never could have learned in many other jobs. You'll stand up for what is right and feel good about it. You'll hone your integrity and become a better person too. When people come to you for help, whether at work or in your private life, you'll have a greater ability to help because of the rich career experiences you can draw from. You'll be challenged mightily, and as a result you'll become a better parent, child, uncle, sibling, and friend—of that I have no doubt.

This is one of the most rewarding jobs around. It has been the most rewarding job I've ever had. There are easier jobs, but few will be as meaningful as a job in the compliance profession. I've learned many interesting and great lessons about the compliance profession—enough to fill a book. In fact, those interesting and great lessons fill *this* book. *I can't wait for you to read all about them.*

LESSON 1
HOW TO HANDLE "THE BIG ONE"

t's clear that the person I'm sitting across from at the conference table is upset with me. He's not just upset; he's *furious*. A few other people are in the room too: my employee and his boss. However, from the moment we started this discussion, it was clear that the very angry and intimidating man was on his own. I just needed to hang in there.

This was early in my compliance career, and on that day I clearly explained the problem my compliance department found to the person who created the problem. He grew more and more upset as he listened, realizing the problem was rather large and he was sitting at ground zero. On top of that, I didn't appear to be going away anytime soon.

"We have to fix this problem, and it will have a material financial impact on you and a few of your colleagues," I told him.

The "fix" would involve refunding a large amount of money to insurance companies due to billing errors. Of course, the man I was speaking with was mad. He didn't like being told what to do. He also didn't want to refund any money. What really made him mad, though, was the fact that his future income was going to drop, because he could no longer bill for as much as he had been billing. This was a very large sum of money.

And *that*, my friends, was when the real party started. He began a rant that would go on and on for some time. Was it pure intimidation? Bullying? Verbal harassment? I'm not sure how to describe it, but I knew that it was just a scare tactic meant to distract from the real problem. Rants like that one are common in the compliance industry, but they're not all the same. Some people intimidate and bully others without any visible antics. Freakishly manipulative people who are smart, have little integrity, and remain visibly calm can be far more dangerous in the long run than the guy I dealt with that day. But guys like the one who was in front of me are far more painful—common bullies accustomed to getting their way due to having a little power. He could bully people, because no one stood up to him. Well . . . at least, not until that day.

The rant went on and on, while I sat and listened . . . *and* listened . . . *and* listened some more. I listened and I paid attention, waiting to hear anything relevant to the investigation we were conducting. One of the insults I heard was: "You're incompetent!" Was it offensive? *Yes*. Was it relevant to our investigation? *No*. Sure, I could have responded and probably *should* have responded in the eyes of many. But I was not focused on defending myself; I was going for the win. All I cared about was defending the facts.

INSIDE "THE BIG ONE"

I heard more insults, yet I heard nothing that would counter the facts I had discovered, which were bad for him. I sat still and looked forward. I didn't blink. I didn't change the expression on my face. It was something like the look you would have on your face if you watched paint dry for 20 minutes. I had no reaction on the outside, but I was caught up in "The Big One" on the inside.

Some cars escape a "Big One" NASCAR crash, and you can escape a "Big One" compliance issue too. You just need to be the calm one in the room.

"The Big One" is a reference to an accident that occurs at NASCAR's faster tracks. Fan or not, you have probably seen "The Big One." All the national news programs show it after the race, because the press and society are enamored with failure. If you haven't seen it, it goes something like this: around 30 to 40 cars race nose-to-tail three-cars-wide at 200 miles per hour. One car up front zigs when it should have zagged. This sets off an accident that involves as many as 15 to 20 cars, all of which get some kind of damage. Occasionally one car flies into the air and rolls down the track, shedding all kinds of things that are important for the car to function properly—tires, body parts, axles, and occasionally the motor. Smoke billows, fires flare, and sparks fly everywhere. Drivers behind the wreck can't see where they are going because of the smoke, and they crash too.

Moments like that rant were one of "The Big Ones" a compliance professional occasionally runs into. It's one of those times in an organization's history when a compliance professional has to make a choice—either stand up and personally take the negative consequences of pointing out misconduct or run for your life and let your organization face bigger consequences later.

The man I confronted continued blowing more smoke and ranting, and I continued listening but not reacting. *If I do this right I will come out the other side a bit dented up, but OK*, I thought. It was just like something else that happens during "The Big One"—something that the press rarely talks about. Look very closely at the crash and you will see one or two cars miraculously dodge about 15 crashing cars. They weave left and right, and then they emerge out of the smoke unscathed. They keep going past the crash and around the track, sometimes all the way to victory. You could be that driver in your organization—the person who emerges out of the smoke and goes on to a compliance victory.

As the beating continued, I realized I had no real backup in the room, but I *did* have help. My boss watched my work from a distant vantage point and gave me advice from time to time. He was my spotter. When "The Big One" occurs, all drivers have an earpiece in their helmets. At the other end of that earpiece is a spotter. A driver's spotter stands on the rooftop of the stands, sees everything, and calmly tells the driver to zig or zag as "The Big One" unfolds in front of them. Good spotters in an organization have a high emotional IQ, stay calm, and can see obstacles in your path before you do. They peer through the smoke that people without integrity put in your way.

The rant wore on. He didn't just say *I* was incompetent, he said my employees who had conducted the investigation were incompetent. One of them was in the room with us. She sat quietly through all his insults. This wasn't her first rodeo. You'd think that I would've come to her defense right at that moment. I was tempted, but I knew that the best way to make her happy was to fix the problem by winning the war, not just this battle. So I stayed silent, despite a million little voices in my head rationalizing why I should do otherwise.

CHANGING THE GAME

The employee in the room with us was there to provide technical support while I described the problem and what we were going to do about it. She knew the facts, but I also selected her from a group of many technicians because she had a high emotional IQ. She could stay calm, even while being called incompetent. She had been an employee there for years. I was the new guy: her new boss and the organization's first compliance officer. I would love to have known what was going through her mind during the meeting. She was probably thinking: *Hey Roy, buddy, I know you are new here, but this is the point at which we apologize, drop the investigation, and walk out of the room. Shouldn't we be leaving now?* She was a great employee, but she'd been taught that when powerful people tell you what to do, *you do it* . . . even if it's very wrong. It was the mid-90s and corporate compliance and standing up to powerful people wasn't as big a thing yet. I was accomplishing many things while sitting there watching the paint dry on the walls of the meeting room. One of them was letting my employee know that the game had changed. What I really want to believe is that she was smiling on the inside while looking stoic to the room. I hope she was thinking: *Damn, this is really happening. We are really going to fix this problem. Roy isn't backing down.*

My employee and her coworkers had raised the issue three years earlier, but were told to bug off. When the problem was first found, there was no compliance and ethics program in place. And no one had the independence and authority needed to fix the problems they found. That all changed the day leadership decided to implement a compliance and ethics program and appointed someone to the compliance and ethics officer position. I was given independence and authority. And the very top person in the organization had my back.

After what seemed to be an eternity, the yelling stopped. The man who had caused the problem really hadn't looked at me much up to this point. He looked at his boss and my employee the whole time. It puzzled me at first. I suspect he didn't look at me because I wasn't visibly intimidated. People, like this bum, want to see the intimidation in the faces of the people they're attacking. They become uncomfortable with you if there is no fear in your eyes. I, on the other hand, was playing a small game with him as I waited. Unless he started sharing pertinent facts, I could play my game, which was to piss him off as much as possible by not letting him get my goat. I liked my goat. I had raised that goat from birth. I was bound and determined not to let him have the goat he so desperately wanted. It distracted me from the pain and kept me from falling down his rabbit hole of inappropriate behavior.

> ## ROY-ISM ""
>
> **Money, power, and influence are no match for a high emotional IQ and the facts.**

At the end of the rant, he looked straight at me with a puzzled look on his face. I had worked around his type for years. They were used to getting their

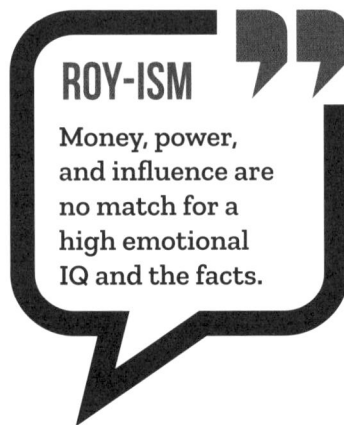

way. He wasn't getting his way. He had the look I was going for—a look that said: *This isn't working. Why are you still here? Why aren't you running away or yelling back at me? Please say something inappropriate enough for me to make you the problem and give leadership a diversion from my problem.*

All I can remember about the very end of this meeting was that I held up. I did not say anything he could use against me. I didn't give him what he wanted and I held onto my integrity.

> ## ROY'S RULE
>
> **Stay focused on the problem, don't react, and never back down, even in the middle of "The Big One."**

GOING BEYOND ETHICS

You may be wondering how that story ended. It was a long process that took months to get the compliance committee, leadership, and others on board to fix the problem. It took a while, but we fixed the problem and corrected the mistakes the man had made over the past few years. As a result, the compliance department gained a little street cred. Others in the organization took notice that things were changing. My guess is a few other problems fixed themselves. People responsible for those mistakes saw that I would not back down—I would get around to them eventually. My employees, who had been run over for years, were feeling a little full of themselves.

Implementing compliance and ethics programs is not rocket science. It's primarily an issue of using tools that have been around forever and mixing in some strong interpersonal skills and strength. If unethical bullies meet up with high-integrity cowards, the unethical bullies win. If they are confronted by high-integrity people with strength, then the unethical bullies lose. It's just that simple. What is rocket science are the interpersonal skills and strength needed to hang in there and fix the problem despite occasional resistance.

The negative culture caused by unresolved problems took a big hit that day at my organization. We had gone beyond ethics and crossed over to compliance. We had gone beyond just talking about doing the right thing to finding and stopping people who were doing the wrong thing. The culture improved and not because we had cool ethics posters, a CEO video saying we were an ethical company, or a code of conduct signed by all employees. All of that is very important, but the culture got a little better that day because we did more than just talk—*we took action.*

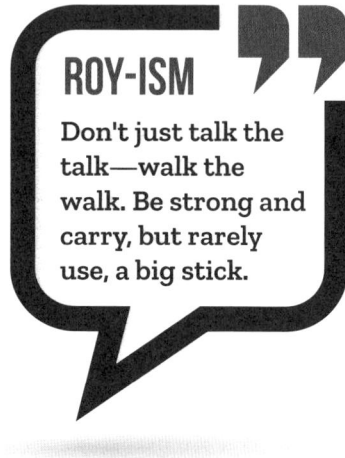

ROY-ISM

Don't just talk the talk—walk the walk. Be strong and carry, but rarely use, a big stick.

10 PRINCIPLES OF BEING A COMPLIANCE PROFESSIONAL

1 **Implement** all elements of a compliance program.

2 **Respond** to concerns and complaints related to ethical and legal violations.

3 **Never compromise** when faced with resistance to fixing a serious problem, and don't overreact to small problems.

4 **Remain unbiased, un-conflicted, and neutral** during problem investigation and resolution.

5 **Have independence, authority, and responsibility** for finding and fixing legal and ethical issues.

6 **Report resistance** to resolving significant issues and impediments to implementing a compliance program.

7 **Ensure compliance problems are fixed,** rather than just advise they be fixed.

8 **Delegate to other departments** elements of a compliance program without giving up authority to ensure compliance-related tasks are completed.

9 **Facilitate support** for the compliance program from leadership, and communicate that support to employees.

10 **Collaborate with leadership** to resolve problems in as positive a manner as possible.

LESSON 2
FILL EVERY HOLE THAT THE RATS MIGHT GET THROUGH

I once walked into work with a belt and suspenders on. Marc said, "So you're a belt *and* suspenders kind of guy?" I really didn't get the point/joke he was making. Later I figured out that if you have suspenders on, you don't need a belt. He was giving me the business in a fun-loving way, but as I write this I realize he was wrong—*very wrong*. The fact that I was wearing a belt *and* suspenders was brilliant. In fact, I should have had rope, some glue, and duct tape holding up my pants. I should have responded, "What? Are you kidding? You taught me to do this." You see, Marc always threw the kitchen sink at a high-risk area.

This lesson eventually became one of the keys to the success of our compliance program. We threw many solutions at a problem at the same time. Marc's solution to potential high-risk problems involved carpet-bombing, just like the enforcement communities carpet-bombed organizations with settlements and corporate integrity agreements. He talked with people who went through what he was about to go through. He didn't just take the best of the good ideas— he simultaneously implemented *all* the good ideas he could find. He surrounded high-risk potential problems with many solutions. He filled every hole that the rats might get through.

My next office . . . filled with all the tools I could ever need.

USING *ALL* OF YOUR COMPLIANCE TOOLS

Here's an example. We needed to provide compliance training to 600 prominent and powerful people at our company. We knew many were going to refuse to come. Rather than send out an announcement for a few session times they could attend, we inundated them with reminders. To start, I went to the compliance committee, which was partially made up of the peers of the people we needed to train. I got them to agree to make the training mandatory, otherwise many people wouldn't come. They all quickly agreed that even if we made it mandatory, many wouldn't come. I told them that some organizations fined people who didn't attend their compliance training, and even gave them evidence of what those organizations did. The committee chair asked what the fine should be. One person suggested a ridiculously low fine of $50.

"Thank you for the suggestion," the chair said, "but Roy and I will work something out."

> **ROY'S RULE**
>
> **Use all the tools you can to fix a compliance problem.**

We met and he asked what I thought it should be. The most I had ever seen was $1,500. I was afraid to suggest that, so instead said $500. He said, "I was thinking $1,000." It was at that moment that I realized that the guy we picked to chair the compliance committee was going to be perfect. "Heck yes," I told him.

Next we sent letters and announced session times employees could choose from, but held off on mentioning the fine. We were going to bend over backwards to take away all excuses for why they couldn't attend. We set up more than 60 different sessions in several geographic locations at all hours of the day. By setting up so many sessions, employees couldn't say there wasn't a convenient time available. And then we started sending out reminders. We sent *many* very nice email reminders about the upcoming training sessions. We also had attendees sign an attestation stating they were there. Some people were mad. I got one attestation in an envelope and it was all crumpled up into a ball. That employee thought he would anger me in some way. All I did was unfold it and file it. Of course, a lot of people came without much fuss. But with a group that big, we knew we were going to get some resistance.

Then we got down to a certain number of people who had not attended. We thought it was time to mention the fine. So we sent the letter that said: "If you don't attend a session by [date], you will be fined $1,000." Next, we reported back to the compliance committee. As we looked through the list of people who received the letter, I blurted out without thinking, "Oh no, we sent a letter to the CEO."

At first the room was silent. Then a couple people on the committee smiled and someone said, "We can't show favoritism. This will be awkward, but this is just the kind of message we want to send."

The committee chair turned to me and said: "Maybe you ought to go talk to him, Roy?"

PUTTING LEADERSHIP IN A BULLETPROOF VEST

I was ready. So I went to the CEO's office and said, "We need you to go to the training."

"I've heard this information presented in several meetings leading up to this training," he told me. "Why would I need to hear it again?"

"You don't need to *hear* it again," I said, "we need you to be *seen* there and we need to be able to say this applies to everyone. Additionally, and as important, if we ever get investigated for anything, enforcement officials will ask for proof of effort.

They will specifically check our training to see how hard we tried. They need this information to determine how big a message to send us—the size of our fines and penalties. Part of my job is to serve you personally. You need my advice. I can't have your name missing from that list. If anyone ever asked how a problem occurred on your watch, I need you to not be the problem."

What I needed to do was put my leadership in a bulletproof vest. The company paid me to educate, audit, monitor, set up a hotline, and, in part, keep leadership out of trouble. Talking with him worked, and the CEO went to the next session. After a great deal more fuss, every one of the 600 people went to a session and signed an attestation. And I do believe that for the last couple of holdouts, we went to their offices and said, "Sit down, please . . . we are doing the training right now."

Do what we did to get our training done—plug every hole the rats can get through and win. Some people might say I bent over backwards and went too far. They are right . . . *and I won.* People who think I went too far are going to have a government investigation someday. Enforcement officials will ask for proof of effort. They will most certainly ask for training records and proof of attendance. Mostly, they'll want to know if you tried hard. And from what I've learned, going too far gets the job done.

ROY-ISM

Win the game! Don't get lost in the weeds.

LESSON 3
STUDY YOUR FAILURES TO FIND A BETTER WAY

I t was just a couple days past my 17th birthday and my buddies Mike Johnson and Tom Kelch (Mad Dog) were driving with me down a dirt road in the dark. My parents thought we were going to a football game. Instead we were on that long stretch of road, one perfect for joyriding. The car was my stepmother's—an 11-year-old Delta 88 with only 11,000 miles on it. It was, for the moment, in mint condition.

"Isn't this where we're supposed to go fast?" Mad Dog asked.

I was only going around 25 miles per hour, and since I had to be reminded, I decided to go faster than we'd ever gone before. I hit the accelerator and got up to 85. The road was straight, but it had hills. When we went up over a rolling hill, we got off the ground a little. After what turned out to be the last valley of our little joyride, we came up the hill and there was a car in our lane. It was very close and *it was not moving.*

Luckily, I reacted quickly and got us out of that lane, or there would have been carnage of unimaginable proportions. However, I couldn't keep the car in the left lane and we drifted into a ditch with two large oak trees and one rather small one. The windshield filled with branches and leaves. We just sideswiped the larger trees, but we weren't so lucky with the smaller tree. We hit it, then the car spun completely around and stopped.

A Delta 88, similar to my stepmother's car

"Get out, it's going to burn!" Mike yelled.

It wasn't going to burn, but we were all scared. I got out, walked about 10 feet, knelt on the ground, and put my head in my hands. The other car's headlights illuminated me and my "oh crap" moment for dramatic effect. Then we assessed our injuries. None of us had been wearing seatbelts. Mike (an athlete) had put his hands on the dashboard and planted his feet on the floorboard. Remarkably, he did not hit anything. Mad Dog bounced around in the back with flying car parts and lots of tiny shards of glass. He rolled up his sleeve and his arm was red with blood, but didn't have any deep cuts. Me? I decided to stop my forward momentum with my face, which slammed into the steering wheel, causing a tooth to go through the skin below my lower lip.

Eventually a tow truck arrived with a police officer. He asked, "How much have you had to drink tonight, Roy?" I said, "I just totaled my stepmother's car. I almost killed two friends.

I have had nothing to drink. Give me a break." It was the truth, however, I probably could have handled that better. Funny thing was, he kept writing and he never questioned my statement in any way. Then the tow truck driver gave me and the guys a ride home.

FACING MY FATHER

There was a party going on at our house, and when I entered, a woman I didn't know walked by. The look of horror on her face indicated something was seriously wrong with my face. I asked her to get my father and then looked in the mirror to my left. There was a small hole below my lower lip, dried-up blood on my chin, and blood all over my shirt. I had what was in reality a small injury, but it *looked* very bad. Then my father walked up.

"I wrecked the car. Everyone's ok. I think I may need stitches. Maybe we ought to go to the hospital," I said. We did and I ended up getting a few stitches. Then we assessed the car—it was totaled.

The next morning I came downstairs and my father said, "Go get me a gallon of milk." He never said a word about the stupidity of my actions.

"I'm not driving anywhere," I told him.

"*Go get me a gallon of milk,*" he told me again. He said it in a way that resulted in me going to get a gallon of milk. He had never sent me out for any grocery item before.

It was unbelievable. He understood what I needed at that moment—to be told to get back in the car again and drive. What I didn't need was to be told I had made a huge mistake.

My dumbass-o-meter was pegged in the red zone. What I learned that day really had nothing to do with almost killing people and wrecking a pretty nice car. I learned a lesson for the ages: *you do not always need to discipline*. It's something I took with me into my compliance and leadership roles. That car-wreck-of-a-lesson taught me why understanding is so important, especially during the toughest moments in a person's life.

I didn't always immediately understand my father's lessons, but he always knew the right response. He taught me one that stuck with me my entire compliance career on the day of that crash.

MISTAKES ARE ALWAYS OPPORTUNITIES

As a compliance professional you will see people make many mistakes. In fact, *most* people at your organization will make mistakes. Dan Roach, chief compliance officer at Optum 360, has even said he doesn't want employees who never make mistakes. "I'm a firm believer that the only people who *don't* make mistakes are those people who don't do anything," Dan said at a 2012 Compliance and Ethics Institute (CEI) session. "It's *easy* not to make a mistake if you're not getting anything done. It's *hard* not to make a mistake if you're actually getting something done."[1]

This kind of perspective helps compliance professionals view employees not as good or bad people, but instead as people who make good or bad decisions. Dan is amazing at responding to peoples' bad decisions. He knows that every person, including himself, has the capacity to make a bad decision. So he always errs in favor of understanding when dealing with people. What's really unique about Dan is that he essentially puts his arm around your shoulder and is very supportive, while simultaneously doling out a credible amount of discipline. Some people get angry or frustrated when they are put in a position of dealing with problems caused by other people. They let it negatively affect their interactions with the person being reprimanded. Dan is as empathetic as he can be, and it gives the people who caused problems the impression that he cares . . . because he does. Dan does this often and he does it well. It serves him well too. It's one of the reasons why he is so well-respected in the compliance profession.

> # ROY'S RULE
> In certain situations, a little bit of empathy can teach far more than a harsh dose of discipline.

Like Dan, good compliance professionals should see mistakes as opportunities. The biggest reason why is that you will drive yourself crazy if you don't. We are asked to deal with problems other people create—problems nobody else wants to deal with. While others avoid the problems, occasionally hiding under their desks, you have to walk into the room and sort everything out. I realized long ago that I learn far more from my failures than my successes. Remember that the next time you're involved in a difficult situation.

Things are often bad enough for people who make mistakes. Piling it on is not always necessary. Don't get me wrong, if you make the same mistake twice in my shop . . . my response

Dan Roach, chief compliance officer at Optum 360

is going to be a lot stronger. You make that same mistake a third time and all heck is going to break loose. The key is to remember that compliance's role is to help people not make bad decisions. Problems are always bigger than the people who make bad decisions—so attack the problem, not the people. Implement discipline when you must (and never make excuses for people who make bad decisions), but also help explain the circumstances that led up to the mistake. Compliance issues always involve situations ripe for failure. Without implementing policies or controls to change these situations, the same mistakes will be made by other people. Learn from compliance failures, have empathy for the people who cause them, and change the situations that allow failures to happen. Do so and you'll prevent those kinds of failures from ever happening again.

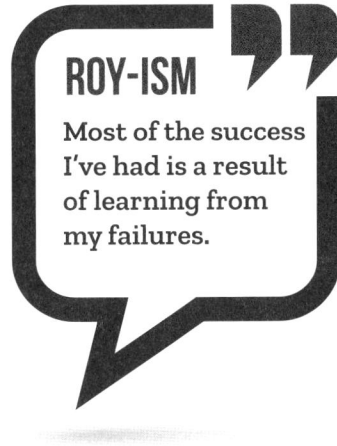

> ## ROY-ISM
>
> **Most of the success I've had is a result of learning from my failures.**

LESSON 4
COLLEGE PRANKS GONE WRONG

"Man, I am going to get you back this time," Larry told me.*

Disclaimer: This lesson may not put me in a good light. But Steven King and Anne Lamott, two writers I admire, said to call upon the not-so-flattering stories of your misspent youth when you write. I misspent a lot more than my youth, so I have plenty of stories. Here are a few that taught me a lot about what it takes to be a good compliance officer.

I was a student at Michigan State University, living in the dorms. With the help of my roommate Tom, I had just pulled a failed prank on Larry, one of my buddies. The failed part was key. I used my failure to my advantage later, when I got Larry back before he could get me back.

I was obligated to participate in pranks. Well not really "obligated," I enjoyed doing pranks—I initiated, embraced, and escalated them. I *loved* to escalate them. In fact I don't know which prank got me into the mess I'm about to share with you, because small pranks were not memorable. The escalated prank was memorable, and the prank we played on Larry was seriously escalated.

The first part started with Larry. I told him, "Hey, you're mad at me and Tom. I'm mad at Tom, because he screwed up the prank.

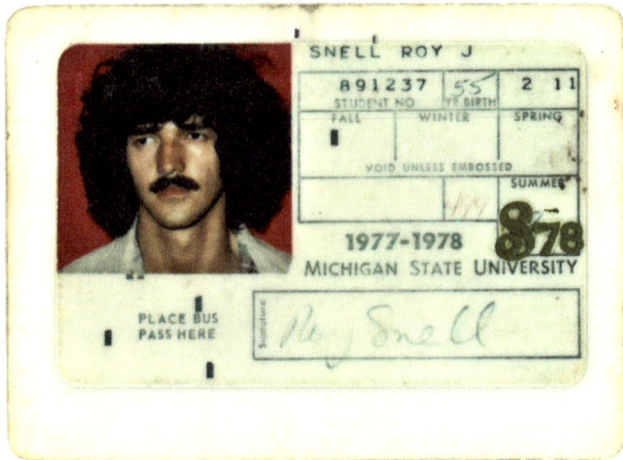

My time as an RA at MSU taught me a lot about dealing with people who've gotten into trouble.

Why don't we both get *Tom* back? Then you can get *me* back."

Larry thought it was genius, but he had no clue it was just a ploy.

Next I went to Tom. I told him that Larry and I were planning to get him back, but what Larry didn't know was that he was going to be pranked again. I explained my plan and Tom said, "Heck no, I'm out."

One thing I neglected to mention was that Larry was a very big dude. I'm 6'2" and Larry was way taller than me. Larry was also built in such a way that I'm pretty sure he could lift half a Buick. I understood Tom's reluctance, but he was key to the prank. So, the prank had to be slightly altered.

My other roommate, Marc, looked a lot like Tom from the back. He was all in from the get-go. Then I lined up seven other guys and we picked a night. The plan went like this: Larry and I were going to go to the cafeteria at about 9:00 p.m. one evening. The room would likely be filled with people who were studying. As far as Larry knew, he and I would load up a 10-inch pile of shaving cream in one hand, cover it up with a piece of newspaper, walk up behind Marc (who was pretending to be Tom), pull the newspaper off, and smash Marc in the face. However, *there was more to the plan.*

Here's what I told Marc and the other guys. When Larry and I were about 20 feet from reaching Marc with the shaving cream, I would yell "Go," rip off the newspaper from my left hand, smack Larry in the side of the face with the shaving cream, and then the prank would proceed as many pranks did—with me running away. But there was more to it. As I ran to the door, with Larry chasing after me, Marc would throw two water balloons at Larry and we would pass three tables with seven guys holding two water balloons each. Each of them would hurl their balloons at Larry as we passed them. On the night of the prank, all started off as planned. Then things went horribly wrong.

A SERIES OF MISCALCULATIONS

I did not see a couple things coming. Larry was big, but he was also fast. I thought that I would have a big lead, but Larry was just 3 feet behind me. This was an important fact that I didn't know. The first problem this caused was not a big deal—Marc could not hit Larry with his water balloons without getting me wet. The more I ran, the wetter I got. I am pretty sure the next seven water balloons hit Larry. The last seven took a while longer to get airborne. The guys had to shift them from their non-throwing hands to their throwing hands. This meant they weren't tossed until Larry and I were well past them. By the time I reached the door, I was soaked. They got Larry pretty good, but also the door, walls, and linoleum floor of the

Ricky Ray Endo (lower right) and I (lower left) played volleyball when we weren't studying or getting into trouble.

lobby. The fact that the floor would get slippery was another miscalculation of mine.

Before I get to the utter disaster part, I have to tell you there was one more Mark involved—Mark with a K. He was stationed at the door and was going to shut it on Larry to give me time to get away. Through the sea of water that flew through the air, I noticed an odd look on Mark's face. He seemed a little surprised, perplexed, and concerned.

I later realized that it's important to read the nonverbal expressions of others, particularly in difficult situations. Mark had information I did not have. Mark sent me a clear signal that something was going wrong or about to go wrong, but I ignored his signals and trudged on with the plan. *Man, I wish I would have reacted better. I wish I would have "listened" to him.* If I had just ran through the door as planned, all would have been fine.

Instead, I thought Mark was chickening out, so I grabbed the outside of the door handle as I flew by and somehow closed the wood and glass door very fast. I did not delegate and trust—I delegated and micromanaged. The door hadn't fully closed when Larry hit the wooden frame, and the entire glass section exploded.

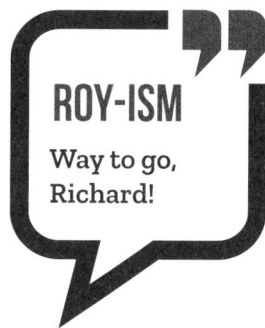

ROY-ISM

Way to go, Richard!

I started running away from the scene as planned, toward the door that led out of the lobby to freedom. When I got to the door, I held it in my hand and paused. If I went through that door, I might avoid being associated with the prank. Instead, I looked back at Mark. He was bent over Larry, who had tiny bits of glass stuck in his arm. Larry had slipped on the water, fallen down, and glass shards went into his arm.

Do I stay? Do I go? I wondered. It wasn't long before I had an answer. Across the lobby from the cafeteria was the dorm supervisor's apartment. She opened her door right then and looked at me. I looked back at her . . . then I let go of that door to freedom. I was going to stay and help make this right. We walked over to Larry, helped him up, and went to the dorm supervisor's apartment. She and I picked the glass out of Larry's arm. I mumbled something about being so sorry, it's all my fault, and some other stuff that she would remember more clearly than I. She did not say much, she just listened. Then I took Larry to the hospital where he got about 20 stitches, if I remember right. Whatever the number was, it got bigger every time Larry told the story. Young women heard 20, then 30, then eventually Larry told them, "Yeah, I got 40 stitches in my arm." I tucked this away in my pitifully empty bin of good things that came from this bad situation—Larry got more attention from the girls. Like he needed it, the dude was an Adonis.

Larry was a little banged up, but thankfully okay, and I learned a few things from the experience that I would eventually use in compliance:

1. I should have expected the problems long before they occurred.
2. Changing plans, particularly during difficult moments in a process, is generally not a good idea.
3. When you see something that doesn't add up, stop what you're doing and start asking questions.

THE STOLEN SIGN INCIDENT

That prank wasn't exactly the only thing I did wrong in college. On another particularly bad day, I was in my dorm room studying when someone flung open my door, saying, "Come quick, Tom is hurt!"

Yes, Tom was also involved in this story. I walked across the hall into the study room, which had been converted around 30 minutes earlier into a boxing ring. Two guys had gloves, all the chairs were up against the wall, and people who had been studying were now cheering on one of the two pugilists. They were until one of them, my roommate Tom, fell backward and hit his head on a chair.

I helped Tom back to our room. Apparently lots of phone calls were made during our short walk, because there was a stretcher, some attendants, and a campus officer waiting for us. And in the doorway was our dorm supervisor, just taking it all in. They loaded my roommate onto the stretcher. Then the officer added to my stress.

"Whose sign is that?" he asked.

Oh crap. I was almost once again through the door of freedom, on the way to the hospital with my roommate—but *no*. The sign he was pointing to was previously above the door of the dean of Agriculture & Natural Resources' office. Now the sign hung mere feet from me in my dorm room.

"The sign is mine," I told him. Well not exactly mine, it was the dean's sign.

Then the officer started reading me my rights. Instead of listening, I interrupted him.

"I have admitted it's my sign. My roommate is being wheeled out on a stretcher. Can we handle this another time?"

It shouldn't have worked, but it did. The officer let me go and I headed out of the room just behind the stretcher. As I passed the dorm supervisor, she said rather quietly (but loud enough for me to clearly hear), "If you need any help, let me know."

My roommate turned out to be okay, but I was later called into the campus police department where I was introduced to two guys wearing dress pants, white shirts, and over-the-shoulder gun holsters—with *actual guns*. They took me to a room with a two-way mirror. Then they questioned me about the sign for what seemed like an hour.

I was expecting a punishment, so finally I said, "Look guys, I admitted to having the sign. I know this is wrong. Why are we still talking?"

"Well, Roy," said one officer, "three days before this sign was stolen, the building it was in was set on fire. Then 11 days after the sign was stolen, the building was set on fire again."

I immediately leaned toward them and said, "You guys have got to believe me. I'm telling you . . . I had nothing to do with that." Shortly after, they stopped asking questions and said the meeting was over. I had no idea why. I was hoping it was because they believed I was telling the truth.

I went back to my dorm and spent around three weeks freaking out before I slowly started to let it go. I was never written up for having the stolen sign and I never heard from the officers again, but this story would come up in a very peculiar way with my dorm supervisor.

"YOU GOT INTO TROUBLE. YOU HANDLED IT WELL."

About six months later, a call went out for people to apply to become resident assistants for the following year. I thought: *I could do that.* So, I applied and went through a first round of interviews. There would end up being many rounds of cuts—down from 110 applicants to seven people for the open positions.

The last cut was a one-on-one interview with, you guessed it, the dorm supervisor. At this interview I learned a lesson I will always remember, have used repeatedly, and will take with me to my grave. I have shared this lesson with many people throughout my career. Frankly, I think it may be the most important lesson I ever learned in preparation for a job as a compliance officer.

The dorm supervisor had seen me at my worst, and I felt comfortable being completely honest with her. I had repeated the standard "I can do this job" answers enough through my many rounds of interviews, and I couldn't continue pretending there wasn't an elephant in the room.

"What am I doing here?" I asked her. "I screwed up and got a guy hurt. I got caught with a stolen sign. You were there! How the heck is it that I am sitting here with you? Why am I still in this process?"

I wanted to be honest and I wanted her to be honest—more than I wanted to become an RA. Man, does it feel good when an honest conversation comes together.

"Well Roy, you got into trouble," she said. "You handled it well. If you become an RA, a big part of your job will be helping some of your guys when they get into trouble. We think they are going to get into trouble. We think you can help them with that."

So, I made the last cut and became an RA, and *I loved it*. I learned a ton about helping people in general and

ROY'S RULE

Be understanding of people who make mistakes and don't write them off forever. Keep watching them, because some people take their mistakes and use them to improve themselves.

especially when the crud hit the fan. It took me years to realize how much my dorm supervisor taught me that day, but eventually I figured it out. I have used what she taught me to help many people. I have made better decisions about people because of her. And I became much more under-standing of people who had problems when I was a compli-ance professional.

As you work with others who make mistakes, remember your unfortunate incidents. What do you have to lose by showing some empathy for others as they go through a difficult audit, investigation, and disciplinary process? My dorm supervisor not only did not penalize me, she put me in charge of a bunch of guys like me the very next year. That seems ridiculous, even to me, but I know she was right to do it. It seems ridiculous only because it's not often done, not because it shouldn't be done. It goes against conventional wisdom. I knew I learned from my mistakes and could help others, because I had been there. She put me in charge of a bunch of college students because I was a screw-up who handled my mistakes properly. I am currently trying to find this dorm supervisor, so I can tell her what she means to me and thank her for her belief in me. I want to tell her the rest of my story, too: *I eventually became a cofounder of the Society of Corporate Compliance and Ethics. I went on to write a book about this sort of thing. You were right to do what you did.*

My advice to you and every compliance professional is to be the dorm supervisor for your company. Try to help prevent your people from getting into trouble, but be as understanding as you can when they do make mistakes. Most of them will mean well—plenty of well-meaning people make mistakes. Think whatever you want to think about the truly unethical people. Hang them from the highest tree if you want. But remember, always remember, the *vast majority* of your people don't know enough about compliance and ethics to be error-free. Embrace your organization and all its flaws, as you should embrace your own. Do it for yourself, your peace of mind, and the people you serve.

LESSON 5
HIT THE COMPLIANCE BULLSEYE WITH EXPERT HELP

"Who is the best?" That's the question my boss Marc Dettmann always asked when we needed to fix a problem. He taught me to respect specialists and how to use them.

When we ran into one significant problem we needed to fix, Marc called our former colleagues at the Mayo Clinic to find out who was the best. This problem was going to rattle leadership like nothing I had ever encountered, and would result in a big financial hit to the organization. We found a lawyer so effective that I have yet to find one better to this day (and I have met a lot of lawyers).

She helped us conduct a big investigation, bringing in other experts when needed. She helped us convince leadership, build credibility, and build a case to fix a problem that some people just didn't want fixed. She explained things to people in such an effective way, that they had to come along peacefully. She reduced the drama that occasionally accompanies these sorts of bigger issues. Between Marc, the lawyer, and I, we fixed a problem that had been met with roadblock after roadblock for several years.

Now there were plenty of things this lawyer didn't know about our specific culture and internal politics, because she hadn't worked with us or in our industry before. So I just didn't let

ROY J. SNELL

Explorer and Author of the Famous Snell Mystery Stories for Boys and Girls

My grandfather Roy J. Snell, who passed on the writing gene to me

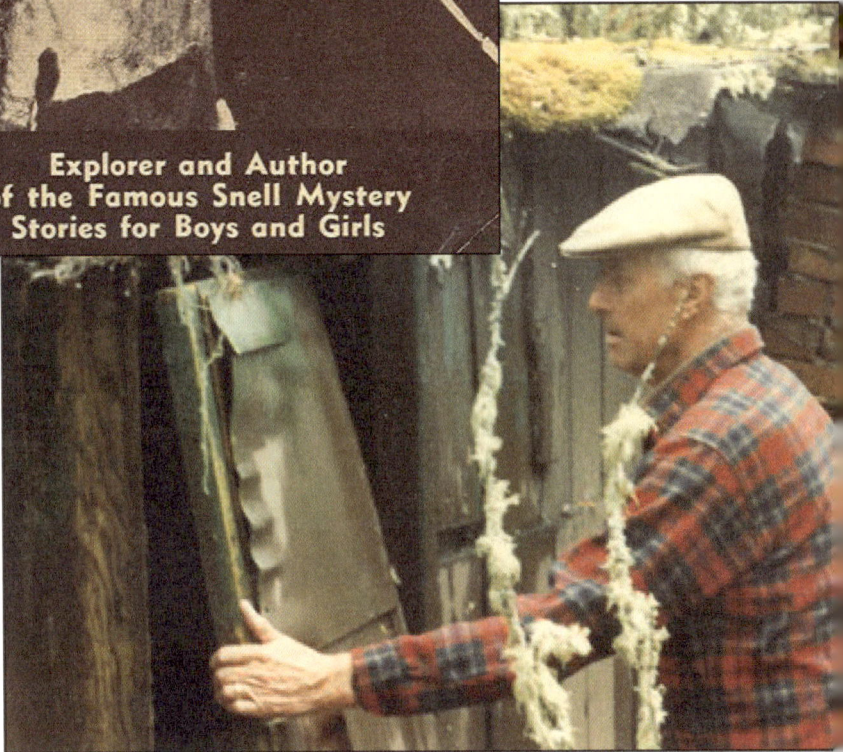

My father by my grandfather's writing shack on Isle Royale

her touch any of those dials on our dashboard. She stuck to what she knew and I stuck to what I knew. And we brought in outside help for the things neither of us knew how to do. *We killed it.*

EXPERIENCE MATTERS

I've learned that experience matters when working in compliance and I'm learning that through writing this book—the first book I've ever written. I've written regularly for many years—a few hundred articles and blog posts—and I know I have the creativity gene. My grandfather Roy J. Snell (whom I'm named after) wrote more than 80 children's books. My mother was an actress and my sister is an artist. This stuff is in my blood. But, I have never written a book before. Luckily, I had some experienced people to guide me: YoGI, our head of publishing, and Karen, my editor. I was convinced this was going to work because I had experts guiding me through the process. YoGI has been in publishing for 30 years, speaks 9 languages, has lived in 11 countries, and I believe he can read people like few others I have ever met. He studied me and, more importantly, my relationship with the compliance and ethics profession. He helped me determine the purpose and mission of the book. I trust him completely. Karen is amazing. Everything I do not know about writing books . . . she knows. I cannot tell you how much I treasure partnering with someone who knows what I need to know and trusting that person completely. Writing this book has been a joy because of Karen. Finding and trusting experts is really important to me.

Working with experts is important for solving compliance issues. Yet some people use just about any lawyer to help them with a high-risk investigation. No one would hire someone who has never worked in a legal department to evaluate their legal department, but many seem to think anyone can evaluate a compliance program and department. I have seen people hire consultants with auditing, legal, ethical, or risk-management experience to evaluate their compliance department. Some have never worked a day of their life in a compliance department. Some have worked with part, but not all of the elements of a compliance and ethics program. *That's not good enough.* We have to do a better job of defining "expertise" in the compliance profession.

Why do you think organizations like Michigan State University (MSU) and Penn State University (PSU) would not step up and stop a known sex offender? Why do you think Wells Fargo CEO John Stumpf listened to employees rationalize setting up bogus bank accounts? How was it that Enron leadership let a CFO build a financial house of cards? These leaders surrounded themselves with generalists who had no clue how bad their decisions were, because they had never been through those kinds of high-risk issues before. Their organizations' leadership did not bring in compliance specialists who would:

- Look them in the eye and tell them the truth.
- Give background facts.
- Cite similar cases.
- Consult and confirm with other experts.
- Provide relevant information to help them make the right decision.

It is dumbfounding to me why many legal departments use their go-to lawyer when a big problem comes up. Some people go to comfort food when they are stressed. I have seen legal departments use their comforting generalist lawyers on high-risk cases. Enron and many other organizations used their outside law firm for unbelievably specialized problems. It's no wonder they got bad advice. Do you think the people who advised MSU and PSU to do nothing for years are ever going to do that again? *No, they won't.* They won't, because they now have experience dealing with sex offenders. This education came at great expense to the organizations they represented.

FINDING THE EXPERTS

Whenever I had a serious problem as a compliance professional, I wanted to accomplish two things that required precision: I did not want to underreact and not address an issue, and I did not want to overreact and fix problems we did not have. That often required getting help from someone who had years of experience in the specific issue I was investigating. Here's an example from one investigation at my organization. I had most of the work done by our staff. Then I brought in not one, but several experts for a day or two each to look at the key findings. I was able to go to leadership with expert confirmation from several people. This made it easy for them to support fixing the problem. Bringing in these experts to review our findings cost very little money. You don't always need to bring people in to do huge investigations that cost a great deal of money. There are other ways to make sure you hit the bullseye and gain the support of leadership.

Finding those experts takes some work though. You need to make an effort looking for them. Get on the internet and start searching. More importantly—start making phone calls. One person will lead you to another who will lead you to another. Then you'll find someone who many people in the compliance world agree is effective. That person will think 10 steps ahead of you and has experience doing exactly what you need them to do for you.

Here's a specific example of the kind of expert you should find. Say you are working on a bribery case. You need a Foreign Corrupt Practices Act (FCPA) attorney who has done all of the following:

- Performed a dozen FCPA investigations in the past several years
- Defended FCPA cases
- Worked with FCPA prosecutors
- Disclosed an FCPA case to the government in the past several years
- Provided guidance to other experts in the field or written or given presentations on the subject

While you're looking, beware of "experts" who aren't true experts. Some people claim to be experts in areas where they have never worked a day in in their life. Compliance is fairly new—it's where the money is and everyone wants a piece of it. Yet just because someone knows *one* element of a compliance program, it doesn't mean that person knows *all* elements of a compliance program. The "expert" might say, "I can do this because I'm a lawyer or an auditor or an ethicist." The real test, though, is whether that person has worked in a compliance department before—*that's* the person you want.

That great philosopher Clint Eastwood once said, "A man's got to know his limitations."[1] Along those lines, I say, "A compliance

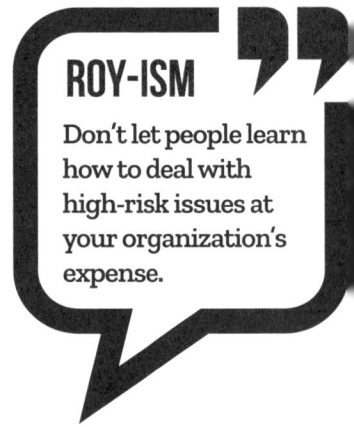

officer's got to know people's limitations." Good compliance officers know this. They respect others' expertise as much as they respect their own and their staff's expertise. They know that experts help them prevent, find, and fix ethical and regulatory problems . . . and using experts will help compliance professionals gain the respect and support of leadership too.

LESSON 6
BUILDING COMPLIANCE AMBASSADORS THROUGH INFLUENCE

L et's start this lesson with a little compliance quiz. First think of the most impressive compliance professional you've ever met. You have five minutes to think and then answer the following questions. *Now go!*

1. Why do you think this person has the right stuff?
2. What kind of relationship does this person have with his/her leadership?
3. Why do you think this person is so effective?
4. What does that person do that is impressive?
5. What does this person do that others don't do as well?
6. What does this person have that others don't have?
7. Did you select this person because he/she knew the rule of law well, could audit like no one else, or did great risk assessments?

Do not proceed until you have a name in mind and answers . . . . Now look at your answers. Do you see a pattern?

I've given this quiz during several presentations and noticed a definite pattern to people's responses. No one ever told me that they picked someone because they knew the rule of law well. No one said the person picked had excellent auditing or risk assessment skills either. What was it that people valued most in a great compliance professional? People skills and the ability to influence others. Nearly everyone said that the person they respected had strong interpersonal skills, had a high emotional IQ, and could negotiate and collaborate well with others.

Being able to influence others is critical in compliance. Just look at what happened at PSU and MSU. Their advisors were unable to influence leadership and sexual abuse continued at these organizations for years. Sexual predators were allowed to be around children and young adults. The harm those predators caused affected dozens of young people and their families. Yet, it could have stopped if the right person influenced leadership. Many major organizational failures occurred with a building full of technical experts—experts in law, audit, and risk. These organizations knew about their different problems for years. What finally made the organizations act? Society. The public found out and crushed these organizations for letting their issues go on for so long. What was missing? Technical skills? I think not.

What was missing was someone, anyone, in the room who could have influenced leadership to fix a known problem. Rather than rationalizing doing nothing as others do, an effective compliance professional needs to be convincing—even when the problem seems incredibly difficult to fix. Having the ability to influence others may be the most important skill that a compliance professional needs to be successful. If you're not able to influence leadership, old problems persist, potential compliance issues are ignored, and the chances of new problems occurring grows. Without influence, you may not get the resources you need to be successful. Without influence, an ethical culture won't develop. Influence is critical to almost everything we do in business and life.

Jenny O'Brien and Roy J. Snell giving a presentation on the power of influence

THE SEVEN ELEMENTS OF INFLUENCE

One of the most effective compliance professionals I have ever met is Jenny O'Brien, chief compliance officer at UnitedHealthcare. What makes her so effective? I think one of Jenny's greatest strengths is her ability to influence others. She knows how to build strong relationships. She takes time to get to know and help people in her organization before she asks for their help. She studies people, determines what they need to be successful, helps them get what they need, and then tries to influence them to help the compliance and ethics program.

She and I talked about how important influence is and why we need more education about interpersonal skills in our profession. Then she and a colleague developed a list of the seven elements of influence (see page 59). It is a structured approach to studying and understanding influence, something that every compliance and ethics professional needs to continuously and consciously work on. I presented these elements with Jenny in a general session at SCCE's 2014 Compliance and Ethics Institute. Your influence will improve as you practice each of these elements, however ideally you should work on all of them over time.

Mastering the art of influencing others takes time and it takes work, but it makes the job of a compliance professional much easier to accomplish. And as Jenny said at the end of the session we presented, "Influencing isn't a one-time thing. We can't just influence when we want to get something done or we want to influence someone, so then we say, 'Oh, today I'm going to influence.' Influence is something we have to do and think about in each interaction, very intentional, strategic communications of what we're doing. [We need] to look down the road and say, 'If I want to get here, what are some of the steps that I need to be doing to build up to that at this time.'"[1] That's what Jenny does every day as a compliance professional.

Take her sage advice. You'll see that when you are able to effectively influence others in your organization, your advice and information about an issue will be *heard*—and they'll be heard from not only you, but also others in the organization who've become compliance ambassadors through your influence.

ROY'S RULE

Interpersonal skills can make all the difference when gathering facts and influencing others.

THE SEVEN ELEMENTS OF INFLUENCE

LEVERAGE
- Vision and Implementation
- Value Proposition
- Empower Others

COLLABORATION
- Know, Acknowledge, and Use Skills of Others
- Let Others Give What They Can and Fill in Gaps
- Document Roles, Tasks, and Expectations

STRATEGIC THINKING
- Bring Strong Evidence
- Stay Focused on Mission
- Consider ROI of Every Effort

COMMUNICATION
- Know Your Audience
- Objective vs. Subjective
- Be Relevant

NEGOTIATION
- Don't Talk—Ask Questions and Listen
- Determine What They Need But Didn't Ask For
- Compromise—Give More to Both Sides and Drop Sticking Points

BUILDING RELATIONSHIPS
- Rapport and Trust
- Investment of Time
- Likeability and Reciprocity

EMOTIONAL INTELLIGENCE
- Self-Awareness and Humility
- Measured
- Optimism, Curiosity, and Passion

SUPPORT LEADERSHIP WITH *ALL* THE FACTS

A big part of influencing leadership is to have as many tools as possible to back up your argument. You need to have *all* the facts—not just a few cherry-picked ideas that support your argument. Giving your leadership the entire picture of an issue is critical to making an objective plan of action to fix the problem.

During my time as CEO and a compliance officer, I kind of knew how things worked or didn't work. I spent 20 some years watching people try to make decisions for our organization without all the facts and then come to bizarre conclusions. It was probably the most frustrating thing I had to deal with. As CEO, I had many people come to me with their hair on fire about something and I reacted quickly and strongly to support them. Then I was told some very important fact my employee left out. I looked silly. I looked ill-informed. I looked like I overreacted. So, if you think your CEO is being unsupportive—maybe you are not providing your CEO with all the facts.

The thing that helped me the most in all this influence, fact-gathering, and decision-making, was consulting with others. I would find someone (maybe several people) unafraid to speak the truth to me and ask what they knew or thought about the facts and the decision I was going to make. And this is key: *I would listen to them.* If what they told me didn't feel or sound right, I would talk to more people. If the stakes were very high, I would search the country for people who had been through that kind of issue before. For the most important decisions, I hired an expert to analyze the information gathered by my compliance investigators and come with me to meet and better influence leadership.

Think about what you can do to be a more effective communicator, rather than place blame on unsupportive leadership. Get more information before you try to influence others. Have passion and emotional reasons to help your argument, but also make sure your argument sits on

> **" Listen more, talk less, and be objective rather than subjective. "**

a solid foundation of facts. The facts are your leverage, and you need them to win. Take the time to build relationships with people before you try to influence them. Try to figure out what someone needs, but hasn't asked for. Listen more, talk less, and be objective rather than subjective.

Study those who do this well and learn from them. Pay attention to the subtle things they do that make them effective influencers. When you are in a meeting, briefly stop listening to what the people in the room are saying. Instead, study *how* they are saying it. Think about the questions I asked at the beginning of this lesson to help you study what is happening in the room. Think about who has the right stuff and who doesn't—*and why*. Then pick an influence mentor. Observe that person and think about why that person is so effective or impressive. Then try to emulate some things that person does. You have to stop only listening to the *substance* of the conversation and start studying the *process* of influence.

Influence is not rocket science. It's just hard work. Fine-tune your interpersonal skills before the compliance conversation ever starts. It'll make it so much easier for that conversation to not only be heard, but also have an effect that lasts.

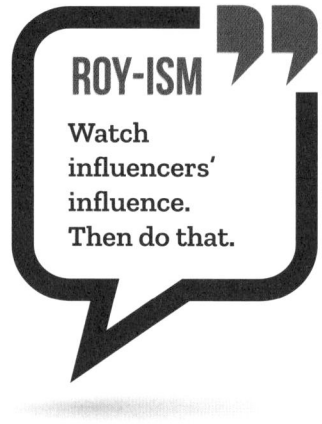

ROY-ISM

Watch influencers' influence. Then do that.

LESSON 7
COMPLIANCE ACTIVISM BELONGS IN A RODEO

I was driving into work one day and got a call from my second-in-command. She was beside herself. The office had been broken into. Computers were missing.

"It's all gone. *Everything* is gone," she said.

I knew we had locked down many of our computers with cables, so I asked her if *all* the computers were gone. Again, she told me that they were all gone.

When I arrived at work, I found that the situation was pretty bad . . . but many of the computers were still there, including our server. It was not nearly as bad as what she had described to me. This person was young and the circumstances were not good, so her reaction was somewhat understandable. Yet after that incident, I was forced to question what she told me. It only takes one bad moment like that to lose some of your credibility, and a number of positive moments to gain it back. It's not logical. It may not be fair. *But it is the way it is.*

I don't know why some people overreact. It's not always caused by immaturity, inexperience, or some other more "understandable" explanation. Some people overreact on purpose. They believe that it is the only way to get people's attention. They're the indignant crowd—people who are kind of lazy, if you ask me. Instead of working hard to try to move things along, they just start screaming, pointing fingers, making exaggerated accusations, and inflaming people. They think most people are bad and most leaders are bad actors who are unsupportive of doing the right thing.

The compliance profession has its fair share of compliance activists: people who overreact to all kinds of situations. It also has about as many who hide under their desks when the going gets rough. These two types of people caused the creation of the compliance profession. They have no place in compliance programs now, or companies will continue repeating mistakes of the past. Most good compliance professionals fall in the middle somewhere—trying not to overreact or underreact.

STOP REACTING, START ANALYZING!

The best thing a compliance professional can do after discovering what could be a big problem is to tell other departments to *stop*—stop writing emails, stop contacting people, and stop reacting. The logic behind this is to encourage employees to have all the facts before making decisions and taking action. *What a concept!* Ironically, many of the decisions made in the minutes after a minor event cause it to become a major event.

There is a place for activism. There is a place for bulls, too . . . and it's not in a china shop. A compliance program is more like a china shop than a rodeo. It may have taken activists to get a compliance program started in an organization, but once implemented and compliance professionals hired, the need for activism diminishes. *Don't get me wrong*, I have been known to light my hair on fire during a meeting to get people's attention—but those were rare and strategic actions. Compliance activists, on the other hand, are just angry with everyone about everything and believe more outrage is the solution to every problem. Instead of calming people down until the facts can be gathered, compliance activists start dumpster fires.

" Compliance activists start dumpster fires. "

I can't tell you how many calls I received from compliance activists when I was the CEO of HCCA and SCCE. They were mad at everyone and everything. They did not contribute one positive idea to the description of their organization, their organization's people, or their situation. It was as if all they did all day was think about how terrible everyone was and how they were going to burn the building to the ground to get their way. They could not tell me what they had tried to do to improve their compliance program.

I offered advice about how they could approach things. They objected to it all, saying my ideas would not work or they already tried those strategies and they failed. They were objecting to ideas before I could finish my sentences. It was obvious to me that they were not looking for a solution; they were looking for someone to complain to for 30 minutes and wanted affirmation for their poor behavior. I was always tempted to tell the truth and say: "You are in the wrong job!" But I didn't because I didn't want the aggravation caused by their subsequent 20-minute denial. I didn't believe they wanted a solution to their problem and I didn't believe they wanted to hear the truth about themselves. All I could focus on was the pain and the anguish this person was going to cause their company, until it ended badly with a sizable payout.

BE EFFECTIVE

ROY'S RULE

High emotional IQ is the key to success for compliance professionals, particularly when there is a major event.

Effective compliance professionals have many arrows in their quiver, and they know when and how to use them. They are not one-trick ponies. They build leadership's confidence in their organization, rather than destroy it. They realize that progress is important, but that they cannot accomplish everything immediately. Effective compliance professionals realize the setbacks caused by activism can suck up valuable, and often limited, resources.

We have a new profession. It's going to take a while to weed out the overreacting activists. If you find someone in your midst like this, work with HR to proceed as professionally and quickly as you can to remove that person from the organization. I have seen people ignore the activism warning signs, put off action, and pay far more dearly later.

When you hire new staff, add as many filters as you can to find the activists and prevent them from getting in the door. Involve several people in the interviewing process. Use personality or work style tests approved by your HR and/or legal department. Emotionally high-strung people are often quite intelligent. In fact, some of the most intelligent people I have met have an emotional IQ problem. They know exactly what to do and say in an interview, but I have found they can't fool everyone and they often can't fool personality or work style tests.

Let me tell you one more thing. It's very important, and it's not going to be obvious. There will be one person on your team who will squint her eyes during the interview process, tilt her head, and say: "I am not sure about this person." My advice: *Heed the warning.*

COMPLIANCE AND ETHICS (PROACTIVE)	OLD-SCHOOL THINKING (REACTIVE)
VS.	
Uses incentives to change behavior	Uses punitive measures to change behavior
Finds core risk areas of a law	Has academic debates about a law
Gathers all the facts for leadership	Gathers information for a defense
Believes compliance protects the bottom line	Believes compliance is a cost center
Uses all elements of compliance	Just tells people to do the right thing
Finds and fixes problems	Finds and passes off problems
Audits affected areas	Doesn't turn over the rock
Does root cause analysis of a mistake	Makes excuses and blames others
Says: "This is a lesson we can learn from."	Says: "We admit no wrongdoing."
Helps operations find another way	Just says "no."
Stands his/her ground on important issues	Goes along and gets along
Independent and unbiased	Defensive and conflicted
Corrects serious problem	Worries about next promotion
Investigates allegation	Questions complainant's motives
Builds ethical culture	Assumes everyone is ethical
Believes education helps prevent problems	Believes education takes away from operations
Disciplines everyone equally	Thinks someone is too important to discipline
Faces the facts	Rationalizes doing nothing

LESSON 8
GET INTO THE SOUL
OF THE MACHINE

Early on in my career, a compliance officer at a Fortune 100 company asked me to come give a presentation on "Compliance as a Verb."

"I would love to do it, but I have no idea what 'Compliance as a Verb' means," I told her. I was honored—I had never received a call from a Fortune *anything* company to come speak. However, I had no idea what she meant.

She explained, "I was talking to your outside counsel. She says you do compliance by walking around and talking to people, rather than just going to meetings all the time." I went from clueless to I got this, instantly.

"I love this subject. I am in," I said.

At the presentation, I basically told the folks in the audience to stop going to meetings, creating spreadsheets, and agonizing over what colors to put in their PowerPoint presentations. I told them to get out and talk with the people who make the mistakes you want to prevent. Get out and talk to people about the kind of culture they want their organization to have. I said they should try to effect change rather than plan to effect change.

I have been preaching this strategy for 23 years and the reaction is always very positive, but then people go back to their office to work on spreadsheets and PowerPoint presentations for their next meeting. I have made a difference in the effectiveness and productivity of others in my career, but at the same time I feel like an absolute failure because people can't seem to follow this advice. This has been one of the most frustrating elements of having to manage people. They want to be productive, but they can't seem to tell the difference between planning to do something and doing something.

SPEND TIME WITH PEOPLE (*NOT* SPREADSHEETS)

Maybe I came to my people-first approach because I hate meetings so much. I believe meetings have a low return on your investment of a compliance professional's time and money. I think the same about spreadsheets, PowerPoint presentations, and other forms of analysis paralysis. I believe most compliance problems are caused by people. So why do we spend so much time in meetings talking to people who already get it and at computers typing stuff few people will ever read?

Part of the reason why the compliance profession was created and why many have failed at it is because leadership and compliance were not spending enough time with the people causing the problems. More importantly, leadership and compliance were not spending enough time with the people who knew where the problems were. When I was a compliance professional we had a hotline that worked like many other hotlines . . . not much at all. Some people would call in to tell us they didn't get a promotion, someone touched their desk, or their supervisor wouldn't let them buy some very expensive piece of equipment. However, we got little to nothing regarding compliance issues. So, instead, I walked the halls. I would walk up to anyone and say something like, "How about them Yankees? Great weather we're having, eh? By the way, are you aware of any known problems that have yet to be resolved?"

One day, I asked someone who worked for me that question, and I'm so glad I did. I had not been there long and so I was not completely aware of all that had happened before I came, and my employees had not come running up to me with their list of problems yet. In fact, I am not sure they really understood how different things were going to be now that we had a compliance program. I asked the question and this very good employee shared with me a big, unresolved issue as casually as the day was long. She and her colleagues had found the problem a few years prior, reported it, and then leadership told them to let it go. She accepted the rejection and forgot about the issue . . . *until* I asked. Without that conversation, the problem could have persisted, possibly resulting in huge fines for the company. Although it took a while, we eventually fixed the problem. All I did was ask a simple question—of someone in the compliance department, no less!

THE STIGMA OF REPORTING

At one point, we had not received a call on the hotline for quite a while. Then it rang, I got excited, and the person at the other end of the phone said, "I would like to reserve a table for four, please." Companies and compliance professionals install hotlines. I am all for hotlines. People need a way to anonymously report an issue. You would be crazy not to have a hotline, because it will help you find some problems. *However*, the number of problems a hotline will not help you find is enormous and you must look for these other problems any way that you can. All issues are not reported to hotlines. Why?

Company culture might be part of it, but it's not the overwhelming reason people don't call you. It could be the result of poor leadership, but that's not always true either. Blaming leadership for everything prevents companies from getting to the real problems and fixing them. When it comes to reporting issues, "the stigma" may be the biggest reason issues are not reported. The irony is that employees are eager to share issues when asked, but believe bringing up issues without being asked is wrong. Of course, some people will complain about anything and everything (and do so on a daily basis), even if they are not aware of any real compliance issues. But the majority of people are deeply affected by the stigma and will not call you.

The stigma with reporting issues on a hotline is that most people think it is essentially the same as "ratting people out" or that it's just not cool. Some blame potential retaliation for not reporting issues. Some people won't call because they believe leadership won't do anything about the problem. However, the biggest hurdle in my opinion is that most people do not want to be a "rat." Yet it's useless to tell employees that calling the hotline is not ratting people out. The stigma is too deeply rooted in our society. This is ironic, of course, because problems go unresolved, and the same people who won't report issues get angry. They ask, "Why won't leadership step up and fix the problem?" What they should say instead is, "Why won't leadership step up and fix the problem I know about, but won't tell them?"

Many people can't shake the stigma. Compliance professionals can tell employees that it's okay to report issues any way they want. Tell employees all day long that they won't get retaliated against. But that does not address what I believe is their number one issue—employees simply don't want to initiate the discussion, but they *will* talk if you ask.

THE POWER OF THE "ASK"

This little secret will help make your compliance program more successful: people are dying to tell you what you want to know. You just have to know how to get it out of them. It's like opening a safe—turn the dial a little to the left, a little to the right, a little back to the left, and then pull. If you just pull on the door without dialing the combination, it won't open. However, with the right combination of questions and a little effort, you can get far more information about problems than you ever imagined. Many people feel badly about not reporting an issue. You just need to let them report it in their own way.

> **ROY'S RULE**
>
> You can wait for the phone to ring and fail or you can go ask people where the problems are and succeed.

If you take the pressure out of starting the conversation, employees feel they have an out. They can say, "I was asked if I knew, so I had to tell them. I'm not going to lie." This trick could get you a goldmine of problems from people who fear the stigma. You are going to find problems early, when they are small. Then you can fix them easily and discipline will be a slap on the wrist rather than a firing.

Seize on the moments when people are particularly frustrated and more eager to share what they know. Maybe it's when they think leadership talks a big game, but won't fix problems. Try this: do some compliance training and emphasize all the stuff that should not be happening in that particular department. You might even get on your high horse about how good the company is and that you believe people are following the rules. Some people in the room will likely know where a problem is, and are going to be a little frustrated that once again leadership is preaching and not fixing the problems. They won't tell you this at the training, though. They'll walk out of that room thinking no one will ever do anything about the problems. They might even be steaming.

A day or two after the training, stop someone in that department and have a private conversation. Comment on the weather. Ask what that person thought about the training. Then ask if the employee has seen an issue mentioned in the training happening in that person's department. You may just find someone who is thrilled you asked. Instead of being concerned with the stigma of reporting, that person will think: *I didn't report the issue. I got asked if I knew of an issue and I wasn't going to lie. Now I have the issue out on the table and I can feel good about how it happened. I am actually relieved.*

GO OVER-THE-TOP WITH ASKS

Now imagine if a few dozen people from the compliance department and leadership asked employees on a regular basis if they knew of any problems in your organization. Think about the message it would send to the employees. People talk about tone at the top. Quite often they just say it's something all companies don't have, and that all leaders are bad. It's the finger-pointing crowd that provide no solutions. However, having many people regularly ask this question and initiate the compliance conversation will do three things: 1. It will trigger complaints that are not helpful to the compliance team, such as, "He touched my desk." 2. It will trigger the discovery of real problems. 3. It will also help set the tone at the top.

Do you think this could be a bit much? Given that the issues we're battling aren't "a bit much," what are we shooting for?

TEN TIPS
FOR HAVING THE COMPLIANCE DISCUSSION

1. Keep it simple.

2. Ask in a casual setting.

3. Ask questions on their turf, not yours.

4. Ask employees at a time when they might be more eager to talk, like after a compliance training session.

5. Talk privately to an employee, rather than with another person looking on.

6. Start the conversation with something innocuous, like the weather or the Yankees.

7. Then ask a direct question, using few words and as directly and simply as you can. Example: "Are there any ethical or regulatory problems here that have yet to be resolved?"

8. If the person mentions something other than an ethical or a regulatory problem, redirect the conversation back to a compliance and ethics focus.

9. Ask people on your compliance team to start these discussions with employees.

10. Ask leaders from all levels of your company to start these discussions too.

If you want people to think there is tone at the top, *you have to go over-the-top*. Ordinary sales and marketing pitches saying you have tone at the top don't work. Ordinary leadership doesn't inspire people. Most would agree with this. Yet, when I suggest actions that may seem a little over-the-top, I hear: "Well we can't do that . . . it's a bit too much." I am sorry, but when you say this, you are preventing success.

Our profession was created to ask those tough questions, find the problems, and fix them before they get too big. Finger-pointing, sweeping negative generalizations, blaming leadership, and blaming company culture are not solutions . . . they're just complaints that won't fix anything. Get down into the soul of the machine and get to know the people in your organization. Initiate compliance conversations. Doing so will help stop the stigma of reporting. If you are willing to study and understand people, you'll get to the root of problems easily. *It's just that simple.*

> **ROY-ISM**
> Go big or
> go home!

LESSON 9
THAT'S WHAT
I'M TALKING ABOUT!

J ordyn walked into my office one day. "I've broken the rule of law," she told me.

The law was the CAN-SPAM Act (which sets the rules for commercial email, giving recipients the right to have an organization stop emailing them). Violating the CAN-SPAM Act can result in tough penalties.

What Jordyn did was purely a mistake. She sent an email message to an email distribution vendor. Instead of telling the vendor to *exclude* the email addresses of people who had opted out of our emails, she asked the vendor to *include* the addresses. So, the email went out to recipients who had specifically asked us to remove them from our email list.

Here's what Jordyn *didn't* do. She didn't try to blame others. She didn't attempt to minimize the problem. She didn't make the excuse that she had to email the vendor hundreds of times a year and state that one mistake was inevitable (which was very true). Instead, Jordyn closed her eyes and owned the mistake. And she had already taken steps to resolve it. She contacted our attorney and listed the incident on our compliance report. I asked a few questions, but she had already taken care of everything I could think of doing. *I was thrilled.*

This is what I'm talking about. As my father used to say, "Good news should trickle out and bad news should travel much faster." It's one of the best pieces of advice I got from him (and he provided a lot of great advice).

At the very next all-staff meeting, I told everyone what Jordyn had done. I explained that as soon as she had done everything she should to fix the mistake, she came to me and told me about it. I told them how she handled her mistake and said that this is what everyone in a similar situation should do. I recognized Jordyn publicly for quickly and capably handling what could have been a big problem.

DEALING WITH PROBLEMS PUBLICLY

The typical reaction to problems is to cover them up and tell as few people as possible—the deny-and-defend approach. The hope is that by covering up problems, a company will suffer less. Ironically, covering up problems does much more damage. Similar problems will likely occur again, because employees cannot learn from a covered-up mistake. Plus, when a covered-up problem is eventually discovered, it results in greater sanctions by the government.

You can buy a pulpit and preach about building an ethical culture or you can actually do something to build an ethical culture. Talking about mistakes is part of actually building an ethical culture. Even if my staff's confessions and my announcement of the mistake to all other staff might have caused more pain, I would do it again . . . and again . . . and again. How many times must we learn from the likes of MSU and PSU that covering up problems makes them worse in the long run? We all agree that covering up problems is bad, but we all can't seem to find the intelligence or courage to publicly discuss them. *That's just stupid.* Disclosing problems sends a message to employees that "we deal with our problems." As CEO, I often recognized

> ## ROY'S RULE
>
> **Within your organization, deal with problems publicly and praise employees who made mistakes and then fixed them. Employees will learn from those mistakes and your organization will have a more ethical and compliant culture.**

people who helped find problems. They are the people who cultivate an ethical culture in an organization. They screwed up, owned up, and fixed their own problem.

Now I suppose there is a limit to all this public discussion of mistakes. Talking to general counsel immediately upon discovery of a problem is very important. However, compliance professionals really have to start working with leadership and legal departments to discuss mistakes more openly. How else will employees know that coming forward with mistakes is okay if they don't see examples of this happening in their organization? The fact that this is rarely done causes employees to be suspicious. It's no wonder employees are reluctant to report issues.

SHOUT IT OUT: REWARDING GOOD BEHAVIOR

I didn't just tell employees about mistakes handled well, I also publicly recognized different employees for their hard work and contributions to a positive work environment. I did this for years. As you do, I also think about the consequences.

This photo was part of a LinkedIn post I wrote about April Kiel—public recognition is part of building a positive work culture.

What will other people think? If I recognize one employee and not others, I could offend people. Now you know why there is so little recognition of people in the workplace. People are too concerned about not offending others. The next time you think there is not enough recognition of people, ask yourself this question: *Am I in part to blame?* Because when public recognition happens, I immediately think: *what about the rest of us?* With that kind of thinking, few get recognized. It's just messed up.

When I recognized people, I shouted it from the treetops. I posted it on social media. I may have aggravated some, but I was doing the right thing. We often don't do the right thing, because it causes short-term aggravation. How can people ever break bad cycles of behavior if nothing changes? Recognize the people who help your organization change for the better—the ones who act ethically and promote a culture of compliance. Speak the truth about mistakes employees make and then fix. *That is what it's all about.*

LESSON 10
SOWING SEEDS OF COMPLIANCE AROUND THE WORLD

Come to Sarajevo.
Help me sow the seeds of compliance in the region.

This short email appeared in my inbox on December 22, 2015, at 8:20 a.m. It was from someone I had never met before, someone living more than 5,000 miles away from where I was sitting at that moment. That email was from Bojan Bajić—a compliance guy from Bosnia and Herzegovina, an eastern European country once part of the Socialist Federal Republic of Yugoslavia. Bojan wanted my help. He wanted to use compliance programs to fight corruption in the Sarajevo Canton—a sector of the country where he lived.

Bosnia and Herzegovina has a long history of corruption. Bribery, money laundering, and organized crime are commonplace. Political corruption exists at all levels of their government. People there lack civil and political rights. There's a social stigma against reporting corruption too. Most believe it won't do any good and, worse, they'll suffer from life-threatening retaliation if they do report the wrongdoing they see. They're right, not much happens when corruption is exposed. Most corruption cases are largely ignored by law enforcement and the courts. The country's corruption is not just embedded in their government, law enforcement, and judicial systems; it's also embedded in their businesses, many of which are still government-owned holdovers from the region's communist days.[1] This post-communist, transitional country was trying to find its way in a freer world. Bojan was part of that change. What he was trying to do there was not just unusual, it was radical—and he wanted me to help.

"Sure," I replied, and pressed send.

Few, if any, folks at the top of the compliance food chain would have said "yes" to traveling across the world and meeting someone they did not know, and some wouldn't have even answered. Yet, when I read Bojan's email, I thought: *these are my people.* I like to help the people nobody else seems interested in helping. I had no idea what was to come, but I'm glad I agreed to help. It turned out that my experience in the Sarajevo Canton was the most meaningful experience of my career.

MEETING BOJAN AND VIŠNJA

After a 13-hour flight from Minneapolis, I arrived at the Sarajevo International Airport and watched my luggage come out on one of the two carousels. Everything there had seen better days. As I stood there, I have to admit I was a little concerned. *What have you gotten yourself into, Roy?* I hadn't really checked into Bojan—I had no idea what kind of person he was. I would later be ashamed of this temporary moment of doubt.

I walked out of the baggage claim and there was Bojan and his colleague Višnja Marilović. They were very humble and reserved, and suggested I follow them to Bojan's car. It was quiet in the car: neither said much. As we drove the streets of Sarajevo, I saw that many of the buildings were still full of

A meal out on my first trip to Bosnia and Herzegovina: (left to right) Rusmir Pobric, Mila Crnogorac Bajić, Višnja Marilović, Roy J. Snell, and Bojan Bajić.

bullet holes from the country's civil war in the 1990s. While we began implementing the first compliance programs in the United States and thought it was tough, Bojan and Višnja were dodging bullets.

They took me to a restaurant for coffee, and then both started opening up. Bojan talked a little, but when Višnja began talking, I was moved like I had never been moved before in my compliance career. It was all a little too humbling to share, but essentially she told me, "I can't believe you came here . . . *to help us.*" She came close to tears. I saw their sincerity and felt terrible for doubting them.

I discovered that Bojan is as charismatic, cool, funny, and smart as they come. His ability to influence others is enviable. Višnja's

Višnja Marilović gave a powerful speech about corruption and her experience as a whistleblower without any protections while accepting SCCE's International Compliance Award in 2017.

integrity and passion for her country runs deeper than most people in the world. Later, Višnja told me her compliance story. She had been working in one of those government-owned companies, and the director was acting inappropriately and unethically. He was taking money and other things of value from the company, and Višnja was the accountant—she knew everything he was doing.

"I saw corruption, fraud, collusion, bribes, and how the company was collapsing together with all the employees and their families," she later said.[2] She wrote to the director and told him that she knew what was happening, from tax evasion to money laundering. She confronted him in person too, but he refused to stop.

"I had a choice," Višnja said, "to leave the company or stay and make things right. To stay and make things right—that was my choice."[3]

She reported the director's misconduct to the government, and as a result, she learned the true meaning of retaliation. She became isolated, discriminated against, and then was fired from the company. She was threatened to the point of needing police protection for her and her children. Soon after, she met Bojan, who was running an organization that advocated for whistleblowers. She told him all of what happened to her when she became a whistleblower and exposed the truth.

Bojan's response was not forlorn, it was very hopeful. He told Višnja: "We will not cry. Let's write a law. We need some law to protect [whistleblowers]."[4]

That's just what they did. Then Bojan, Višnja, and their colleagues convinced eight parliamentarians to support their law.[5] It passed, becoming the first national whistleblower pre-court protection law in the country *and* all of Europe.[6] Over the next six years, they developed a whole compliance program based on the seven elements of compliance.[7] They used the SCCE website as the source of their compliance knowledge. "We read, analyzed, and discussed every word that we found there. We had a deep understanding of the purpose of rules and ethics in business," Višnja said.[8]

THE MISSING PIECE: REGULATIONS

When they offered their program to the businesses of Bosnia and Herzegovina, they discovered a problem: no one wanted to implement their compliance program. So, that's when Bojan contacted me, and that's why I was there—he wanted me to help him understand what they should do to get businesses to implement compliance programs. I explained that they needed regulations to enforce compliance, or few businesses would get involved. I said that the US government had made so much progress because regulators and the enforcement community had made significant effort to encourage organizations to implement compliance programs. With the threat of severe penalties, businesses were compelled to comply.

During the trip, I spoke at their compliance conference and met with the people of the Sarajevo Canton, including some working in the government. Soon after I left, Bojan, Višnja, and their colleagues began working with companies to adopt new regulations to enforce their compliance programs. I came back a year later and met with the prime minister of the Sarajevo Canton and Bojan had already convinced him to implement compliance programs in all 200 companies in the area, most of which were government-owned. I did my best to support them in their struggle to help improve their country and economy, and fight corruption using compliance programs.

A few years later, in October 2017, the SCCE awarded Bojan and Višnja the International Compliance Award for their work in Bosnia and Herzegovina. SCCE Vice President Adam Turteltaub introduced them and described their path-making work, saying that: "Running a compliance program is never easy . . . starting one is harder still. Helping to start many of them in a region without a history of a rule of law, still recovering from a war,

Adam Turteltaub (left) with Bojan Bajić (right) as he tells of his compliance journey in Bosnia and Herzegovina while accepting SCCE's International Compliance Award in 2017.

still getting used to capitalism, and rife with corruption, is a Herculean task."[9]

Adam went on to say that Bojan had vision to promote compliance programs under such difficult circumstances. Choosing his words carefully, Bojan said, "Thank you, Adam, that you said that I had a vision, but in real life, I rather would say that I didn't have a vision. I was unconsciously self-confident. I really didn't know anything about compliance, about investigations, about whistleblowing. Everything happened accidentally. I just was trying to do what . . . was in my heart, what was right to do in the country where compliance was unknown."[10]

> ## ROY'S RULE
>
> Compliance and ethics professionals not only make organizations better, but also whole regions of the world better too.

I don't think I will ever find a better example of an accidental compliance professional than Bojan. Think about his example. People walking the streets of a troubled country trying to figure out how to make it better. Rather than giving up and turning to violence, they start a compliance and ethics program. They were ordinary citizens changing the course of their country one step at a time. It was unbelievable.

THE PUBLIC INTEGRITY ACT

On January 26, 2018, some of us from the SCCE met with Bojan in Washington, DC, to help write a law he was working on for the prime minister. We primarily helped describe the compliance programs to be implemented through the law. We also made a few suggestions about the independence of and reporting structures for compliance officers. They called the law the Public Integrity Act. It was a perfect name.

Then all heck broke loose, which I learned is a redundant statement for things that happen in the Sarajevo Canton. The

The small group who helped write the compliance program section for the Sarajevo Canton's Public Integrity Act in 2018: (left to right) Dan Roach, Leonard F. McCarthy, Bojan Bajić, Odell Guyton, Roy J. Snell, and Joseph Murphy.

prime minister's party decided to throw him out. Apparently they thought he should fight *for* corruption, not *against* it. He left on his own accord to form a new party, called the People and Justice party. I assumed the effort was dead.

In late 2018, I received an update from Bojan. The Public Integrity Act wasn't dead after all. Six political parties joined

THE GODFATHER OF COMPLIANCE:
JOE MURPHY

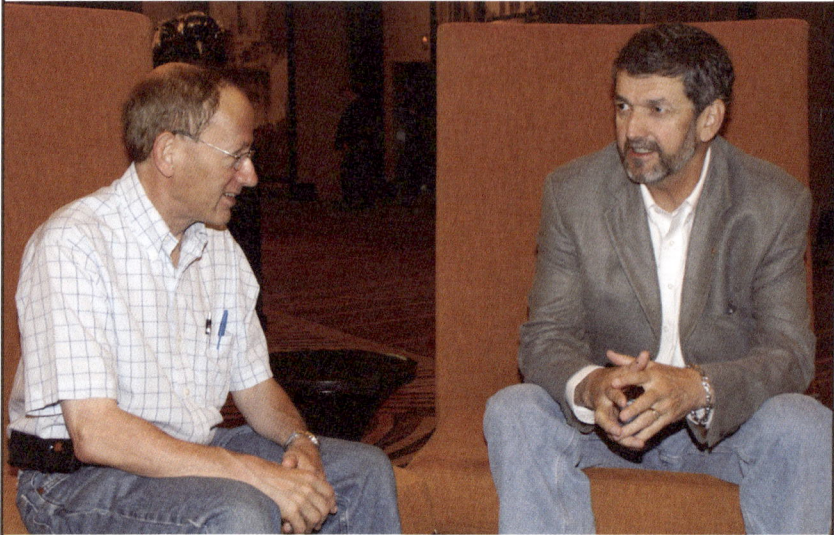

Talking with Joe Murphy, one of my 1,000 strategic advisors

Included in the group that flew to DC to help Bojan was Joe Murphy. I consider Joe to be the godfather of compliance. He was invaluable in helping Bojan write the Public Integrity Act, and he also flew to the Sarajevo Canton at Bojan's request to help him convince business leaders of the benefits of compliance programs. Not only has Joe helped many foreign businesses adopt compliance programs, he has also probably helped more foreign governments understand compliance programs than anyone I know.

Joe's been involved in compliance since dirt. And he's worked harder than anyone else I know to make our profession better. He joined SCCE's board and has given us many ideas to pursue. Joe keeps a low profile, but he's willing to help any person or organization dedicated to compliance. He doesn't care how hard the task—Joe tries to make things better in our profession. He is sowing seeds for our future. And he's become known around the world for his compliance expertise. Joe's the go-to guy for many governments that want to encourage organizations to implement compliance programs. Countries that want to become more trusted and therefore successful in the global economy have benefited from his help. Yet he doesn't talk or write much about his work with other countries . . . and he asks them not to give him credit. He sees a fledgling effort in some far-flung place in the world and writes them offering ideas, content, and encouragement. Many have asked him to come help; I have never seen him refuse. *No one I know has done more for this profession.*

together to form the new government. They hope to pass the Public Integrity Act and implement compliance programs in every business in the Sarajevo Canton.

"You need to prepare your compliance gang to come to Sarajevo very soon to continue the work that we started," he wrote to me.[11] Even better, the new prime minister told Bojan that "the Public Integrity Act will be the backbone of this government."[12]

I'll be headed back to Sarajevo in October 2019 for the SCCE Western Balkans Regional Compliance & Ethics Conference to speak and learn more about what is happening in compliance there. SCCE will continue to work with Bojan and Višnja, supporting their compliance efforts in the country. I'm not sure what will happen, but Bojan is optimistic. He's used to all the chaos and setbacks. That is how things work in many eastern European countries. Bojan doesn't get discouraged for long and he doesn't give up. He is always planning his next steps to make compliance programs commonplace and do what he feels is right for his country.

The lessons we can learn from Bojan and Višnja's experiences are numerous. Have courage. Never give up. Stay and fight for your region of the world rather than abandon it. Never hesitate to ask someone for help, no matter how slim the chance of a "yes" will be. But the lesson of all lessons here is that when compliance regulations are missing, when the rule of law is absent, corruption prevails and regular citizens suffer. Yet, there is always hope for

> **ROY-ISM**
>
> **Be relentless with compliance, even when facing defeat.**

change. People like Bojan and Višnja found hope in compliance and ethics programs, and they are using those programs to fight their monumental problems. *How cool is that?*

BATTLING CORRUPTION IN BRAZIL

Eastern Europe is not the only region of the world where compliance and ethics professionals are trying to make the world a better place. Many of us witnessed a true explosion of the compliance profession in Brazil. My dear friends in Brazil are battling the forces of corruption and many other ethical and regulatory irregularities using compliance professionals. There have been many recent corruption prosecutions in Brazil. Most notable are ones involving the state-run oil company Petrobras, from which spread a worldwide web of corruption exposed in 2014. It was the largest corruption scandal in Brazil—maybe even the world—that involved $5 billion in bribes paid to executives and politicians, kickbacks from contractors, money laundering through car washes and gas stations, and black market money dealers.[13] This international incident involved a dozen countries, including the United States. US prosecutors and regulators joined the Brazilian investigation, and in the end Petrobras paid the United States $853.2 million in fines for breaking US anti-corruption laws.[14] There have been many bribery settlements in Brazil since the Petrobras corruption broke. Some very negative and ill-informed people think that this rise in corruption cases and settlements mean corruption's getting worse in Brazil.

Let me help out these poor confused souls. Brazil is making real progress that should be recognized and encouraged. In the past, Brazil had a culture of impunity—people in power got away with just about anything. There were few, if any,

In 2016, the Brazilian people filled the streets to protest corruption in the country.

prosecutions for bribery. Do you think that means bribery wasn't happening? If you believe that, you need to talk to the people of Brazil and get the facts. First, Brazilians protested corruption, as hundreds of thousands—possibly a million or more—people took to the streets to demonstrate starting in 2013.[15] To appease the public, President Dilma Rousseff fast-tracked anti-corruption laws, including a measure to allow plea bargaining for the first time in Brazil.[16] Then the bribery cases and prosecutions started to come. Now there have been many corruption prosecutions. As a result, those considering taking or giving a bribe will likely have second thoughts or, if they don't, they'll face prosecution. The recent bribery settlements are not a sign of *more* bribery, they are a sign of *addressing* bribery and corruption problems.

Brazil is far ahead of many countries in the implementation of compliance programs and the hiring of compliance professionals. SCCE holds a handful of conferences there every year and has done so for many years. Many Brazilian compliance professionals are certified by the Compliance Certification Board and are members of SCCE. These compliance professionals benefit by the rule of law being enforced.

For most compliance professionals, the higher authority is their board. For Brazilians, the higher authority is their board *and* the court of public opinion. They do have some significant help from the enforcement community, but for the most part, many compliance professionals in Brazil are backed by the good people of Brazil. Their constant protests against corruption and conscientious voting decisions help compliance professionals do their jobs.

Brazilian compliance professionals are using this support and momentum to root out and fix corruption in their companies. Their efforts will build public trust in their companies. They will build public trust in their country. After the country cleans up its corruption, Brazil's economy will soar as it becomes a trusted player in the global economy. Maybe then the critics of Brazil will figure this all out.

Some believe that the SCCE played a small role in fanning the flames of the Brazilian compliance movement. I will never know and that bothers me. I want to feel like we were a part of it. I can tell you this for sure: Shin Jae Kim, who is head of

Shin Jae Kim, who helped start a compliance revolution in Brazil while serving on our SCCE board

the Compliance & Investigation group at the Brazilian law firm TozziniFreire Advogados and a current SCCE board member, has made a huge difference in Brazil. Years ago, Shin grabbed a bunch of us by the ear and dragged us down to teach compliance there. Now what we see there is utterly amazing. Wonderful people using compliance programs to try to make Brazil a better place.

LESSON 11
NIGHTMARE ON THE PAPAONGA RIVER

"Oh no. It broke!" said Gene, my friend Dan Roach's dad.

We were sitting in our boat at the banks of the Papaonga River, which runs through a remote area of Ontario, Canada. It was dark, *very dark*. I couldn't see what Gene was talking about, but I knew whatever broke was really important. This was the most animated I'd ever seen Gene. He was usually such a cool customer—he'd spent his career in mining and eventually became a steelworker's union negotiator. Being a negotiator for the steelworker's union was a long slog through the woods that involved solving never-ending problems. I waited for Gene to speak again and maybe give me a little more information— being quiet right then seemed like a good thing.

Finally . . . "The gas line broke," he told us.

It had been a very long day: Gene, Dan, and I had started traveling at the crack of dawn and now it was the crack of dusk. We were in the middle of nowhere, because Dan and I were looking to buy a remote property in Canada. We looked at many places over close to five years, but the property off the Papaonga River was the one I wanted. However, I wasn't going to buy it without my partner in crime—Dan—who had a problem with the property: there was no road to the lake the property was on. Dan wanted to be sure we could get there without using an expensive sea plane, so we were searching for other access routes. We tried to see if we could walk in from the end of a logging road, but that ended in what I would simply refer to as "the endless swamp disaster."

Now we were trying for water access. After driving on logging roads all afternoon, we found an old overgrown road that seemed like it might head in the right direction. We walked in front of Gene as he slowly drove his truck behind us. Thick brush higher than our heads covered the road and we could barely see 10 feet in front of us. Fortunately the road ended only a quarter-mile from the Papaonga River. From there, we would use a boat to cover the last 5 miles by water to the property. It was very cold and misty, and we were 50 miles from the nearest light bulb, cell tower, or store. We had hauled our boat and supplies from the road's end to the riverbank down a small slippery cliff, through more thick brush, and across a small swamp. But now the boat engine wouldn't start with a broken hose. We were going nowhere, and we were far from help. Then suddenly, Gene had an idea.

"I think I have a short piece of hose in the back of my truck that we could use to fix this," he said.

Hope? I thought, *I'll take hope.* So we headed back up the hill one more time to get the hose. The odds were slim that it would fit though—it needed to be perfect. If any air got into the gas line, there wouldn't be a vacuum and gas could not travel from the tank to the motor. We got to Gene's truck . . . and *there it was.* Then Gene opened his toolbox. It was vintage green, and I swear it had 200 tools meticulously stored like a jigsaw puzzle. From it he grabbed two hose clamps and a screwdriver, and we headed back down the hill for the last time that night.

MAKING OUR WAY,
ONE CHALLENGE AT A TIME

Incredibly, the hose fit like a glove and the clamps secured it to make a tight seal. We pushed off in the boat and looked downriver. Light was fading fast, and we could barely make out the trees from the sky. If there was a moon, it was blotted out by the clouds and mist. We had a flashlight, but I'm guessing the batteries were last changed when Millard Fillmore was president. We were searching for a 30-foot wide inlet from the quarter-mile-wide area we were in—it wouldn't be an easy ride.

Then we noticed a slight V-shape in the trees. We headed toward it, and it turned out to be the inlet that led to the rest of the river. But there were other issues we were worried about. People warned us that rocks and logs were everywhere in this river. We had one motor and one prop. If we hit something, things would go from a very long, somewhat bad day to a real problem that couldn't be solved easily. So, we moved slowly through the water. Luckily, it turned out that the water level was high and all the trouble was just a little lower than usual.

We passed through a small lake, got lost in the dense fog, and found the entrance to the next and, thankfully, last stretch of the river. Finally we entered Papaonga Lake. Now, except for the smallest black dot you could imagine, it was just all dark. We couldn't see the difference between the sky, trees, and water. We were about three-quarters of a mile from the cabin—all we had to do was know where to aim. Dan and I had been studying Google Earth for six months and we had the lake memorized. Gene was steering and asked us where to go. We told him to head toward the very small, even blacker dot. This dot was a small island, basically a rock with a couple trees on it. The dot guided us halfway through the lake, but on the other side of the island there was nothing. I've had my eyes open and saw nothing only a few times in my life. It was unnerving.

Gene calmly asked, "Where do I go now?"

Then Dan and I thought of something: we told Gene to look at the wake behind the boat and keep it going straight. The way forward involved looking backward. About 10 minutes later, trees and a dock emerged in front of us. We had arrived at the end of the dock in front of the property's cabin . . . in total darkness.

It had been a long, hard day, capped off by a two-and-a-half-hour boat ride up a winding river none of us had seen before. It was cold and we were wet, and at 75, Gene was clearly worn out. As I stood on the dock unloading our stuff I was thinking about one thing: *What do Gene and Dan think about this way into the cabin?* But I didn't ask; I waited. We entered the cabin, turned on the solar lights, ate, and went to bed. The next morning we headed out for a tour of the lake.

Out of the blue, Dan asked his father: "What do you think?"

Gene said, "I think we should get this place."

I almost jumped out of the boat. There was no discussion of the effort it took to get there. It had been difficult, but I knew these two guys embraced overcoming adversity. Dan and his dad appreciated what it took to do what we did.

We bought the property and hauled in enough building material and furnishings for three cabins. Almost all of it came down a muddy, miserable trail and up that log and rock-infested river in our 14-foot boats. There probably

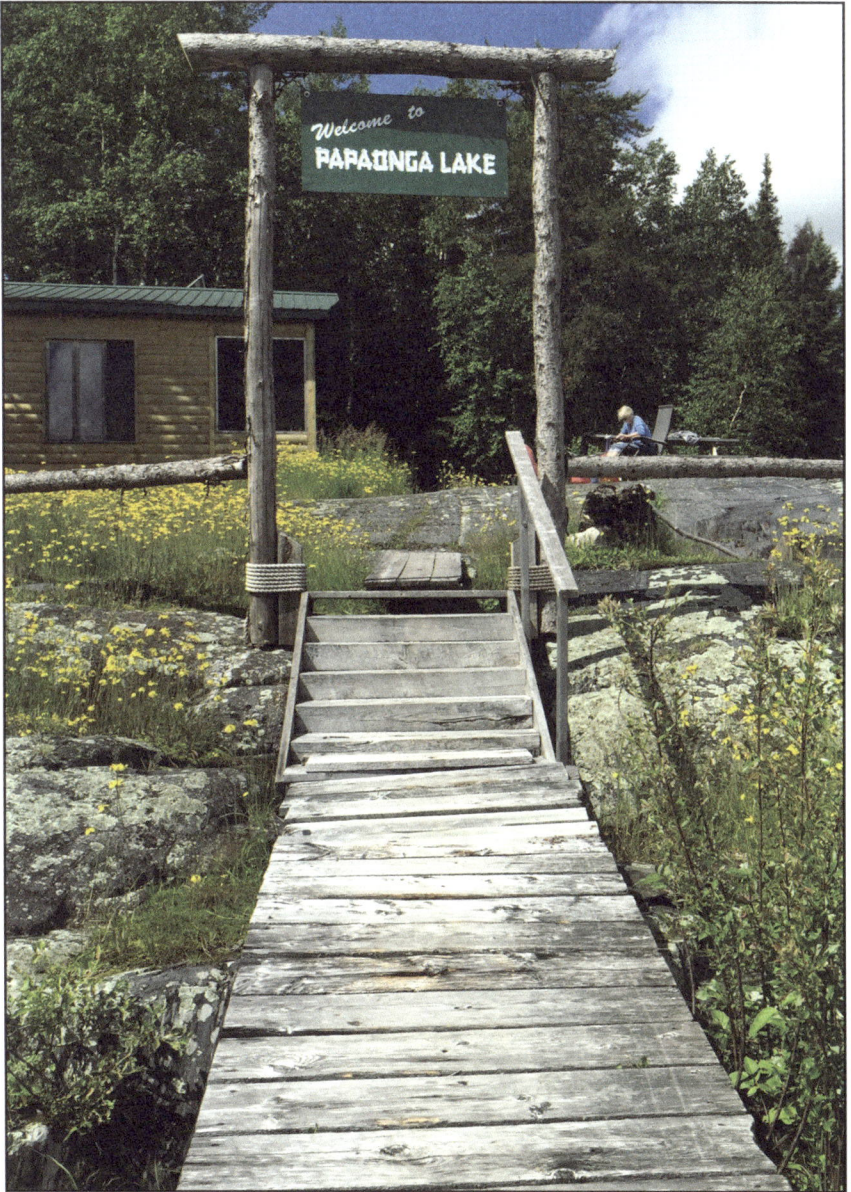

Our dock, the one we found in pitch darkness after a very long struggle in the Canadian wilderness.

was some point along the way that each of us thought of quitting . . . but we didn't. We now all feel so glad we stuck it out. As I write this, we just celebrated our tenth anniversary up there. The joy we have spending time in this remote and peaceful little piece of planet Earth is indescribable.

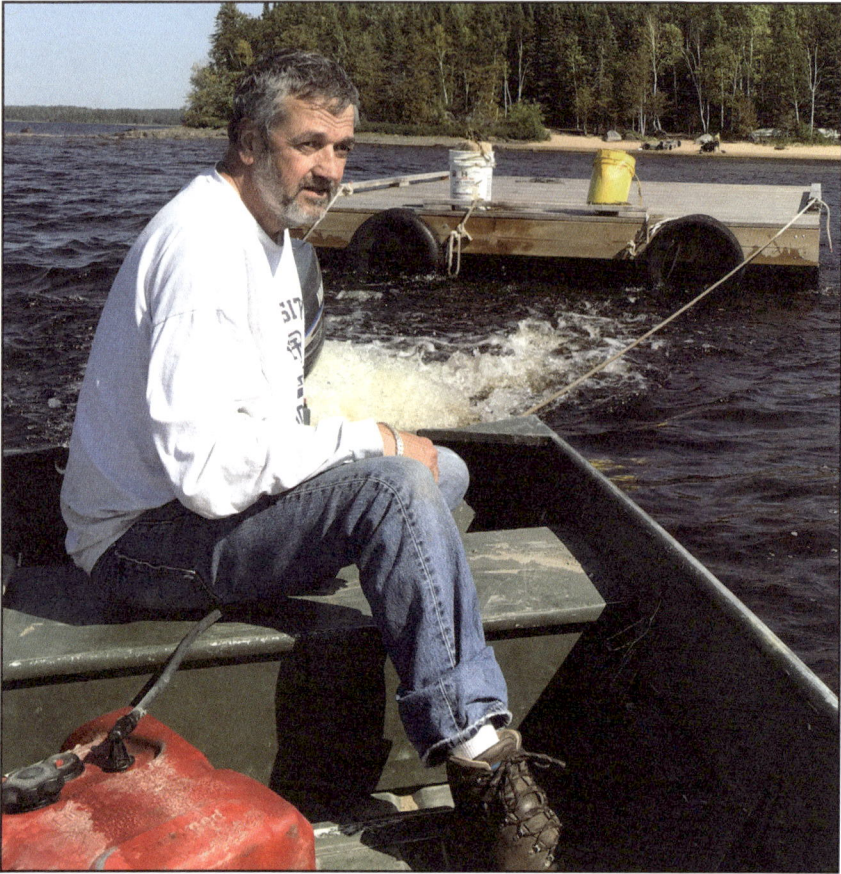

When I am not battling for the compliance profession, I am in remote NW Ontario where there are few regulations.

THE LONG COMPLIANCE JOURNEY

It can be a long road getting where you are going sometimes. I get calls quite often from compliance professionals who see nothing but problems. Many are new to compliance. Quite often their hair is in flames. They blame everyone they can think of for their failures. They are frustrated with how long it takes to get things done. They want a completely effective compliance program overnight. Yet, they encounter hurdle after hurdle and wonder why things are going so wrong.

What I say to them might be surprising: *The problems aren't a problem*. All compliance programs encounter problem after problem. Compliance programs are endless journeys with many obstacles. If your progress is limited, but consistent, you will end up somewhere significant long after you started. I am pretty sure that it is impossible to accomplish anything grand without a long slow slog through the mud. The long journey and the many problems you solve along the way are in the end called "great accomplishments."

ROY'S RULE

Compliance professionals and their organizations need to keep the end point in mind, embrace adversity, endure the daily issue-filled grind, and they will achieve great things one small gain at a time.

On some days when I was leading a compliance program, things got tough for my compliance team. So, I would talk about some of our past accomplishments. When you are in the darkest days, you just have to start spinning. You have to put the best light on the dark situation. That's what all great leaders do and what all great accomplishments involve—dark days and people who refuse to get discouraged.

This didn't happen at MSU, after they had a huge scandal with a male doctor who was abusing young women and children for years. The university hired a compliance officer to implement a compliance program and report to the board. This was the best possible reaction to the failures of the past. Unfortunately, they selected an academic professor from their law school to be the compliance officer. He had little experience running a compliance program and knew little about the compliance profession. Just a few months into the job, the new compliance officer quit. The *Detroit Free Press* reported

Small gains led us to this ideal place in Canada, just like small gains over the years will take your compliance program to a more ideal place in your organization.

that he was stepping down due to "a lack of resources to implement the office."[1]

This was terrible for MSU, but was also bad for our profession. The guy they hired to be their compliance officer did not understand what the challenges of running a compliance program were. He cut and run the minute he had his first problem: a lack of resources. *Are you kidding me?* We all lack resources. Every department lacks resources. This guy didn't see this coming, because he had no clue as to the slings and arrows of running a compliance program. If you want to be a successful compliance officer, you have to care more about doing the right thing than about yourself and the pain of dealing with problems.

JUST WAIT: SMALL GAINS LEAD TO BIG SUCCESS

If you can get people to focus on the journey of implementing a compliance program, rather than on what is going wrong or how unfair things might be, then your life will be remarkably easier. Nobody who knows anything about compliance programs expects you to be done overnight. They just want to see that you are making progress and fixing the problems you find. Frankly, I would argue you will never be done. I believe that most leaders see what you are up against and just want you to hang in there.

When you are in a situation where the endpoint is unknown, and the road to where you are going is littered with challenges, ask yourself:

- Are we successful enough?
- Are we still making progress?
- Are we still improving?
- Are things getting better?
- Are we solving the problems we find?

If you answered "yes" to these questions, your compliance program is succeeding. Remember to focus on the entire journey. Progress is what you are shooting for, not perfection. Small gains over the course of years are what you are shooting for. Those small gains will add up to great accomplishments for you and your compliance team. If you don't quit, someday you will get to a point where you look back from where you came and think: *We did all that.*

> **ROY-ISM**
> Keep the end in mind, but focus on the journey.

LESSON 12
THE DANGERS OF RATIONALIZATION

Writer and philosopher Ayn Rand once said, "Rationalization is a process not of perceiving reality, but of attempting to make reality fit one's emotions."[1]

Psychoanalyst Karen Horney once said, "Rationalization may be defined as self-deception by reasoning."[2]

Someone in compliance once told me, "If you find yourself trying to explain something after you did it—that's rationalization."

I say, "Rationalization is at the root of many bad decisions."

Rationalization is a disease that infects good decision-making. It helps wrongdoing persist. It convinces otherwise ethical people to do or ignore unethical things. Here's a prime example. I posted something on social media about an organization that in the eyes of many people did not adequately address a known problem. It involved child abuse. One employee witnessed a particularly terrible crime. Yet the organization did very little about the problem. The perp continued abusing children and suffered little-to-no consequences until society found out about the abuse many years later. Then all heck broke lose. The organization suffered greatly in terms of bad PR. The perp went to jail, but numerous victims were left to deal with the effects of his abuse for the rest of their lives. Many people who did nothing except help cover up the problem lost their jobs, and their reputations and careers suffered. My post was critical of the organization's handling of what I considered to be a terrible crime and a wildly inadequate response by leadership.

Then an ethicist from that organization posted a comment. It said that I had not studied the facts and there was some question about who knew what when. *I was dumbfounded.* I had studied quite a bit, but that was irrelevant. The organization had an eyewitness to a terrible crime and did little to nothing. I couldn't believe what I was reading—an ethicist rationalizing? This individual was pretty well respected in the ethics community . . . a leader really. If an ethics leader can rationalize an incident like this, we are all doomed—unless we work with compliance professionals who are trained to spot and stop rationalization. It's a big part of why the profession was created. Too many people, like this ethicist, rationalized doing too little in response to serious issues.

WHEN RATIONALIZATION CREEPS IN

If you see the following conditions developing in your organization, be ready to help leadership see what's coming. They often cause people to rationalize doing too little about a known problem. They include:

- ☐ Discovering a very big problem
- ☐ Disclosing the problem could hurt somebody's reputation
- ☐ Disclosing the problem could hurt the organization's reputation
- ☐ Having employees who feel badly because the problem happened on their watch
- ☐ Knowing that the perp is a colleague
- ☐ Believing the perp is an otherwise good person

- ☐ Having leadership surrounded by people who want to help minimize the problem
- ☐ Having leadership surrounded by very smart people who are excellent at rationalization
- ☐ Having leadership that strongly trusts in their advisors
- ☐ Having people involved in the problem resolution who are conflicted

If you can check most of these boxes, be on the lookout for advisors who rationalize doing little to nothing about a problem. Often the strong employees who surround and advise leadership are ironically the most likely to bury leadership when there is a serious compliance issue. Many leaders who decided not to address an issue are good people who had bad advisors, got bad advice, and made bad decisions. I understand there are a few bad leaders who are eager to go down the wrong path. But the idea that all leaders are bad and we can fix all our problems by firing leaders is a big mistake. We have to look at the process. Always blaming leadership is not only wrong in many cases, it prevents organizations from discovering and fixing real problems. When leadership discovers a serious problem, they need to recognize the signs and symptoms of rationalization in the people around them. Compliance professionals can help leadership do this. They must dig deeper into peoples' motives to help figure out how to spot and stop rationalization.

I try to imagine what was said in the meetings that caused otherwise good people to rationalize something as tremendously stupid as not dealing with a known problem. There *had* to have been a meeting or two where leadership discussed the problem. Their reaction was understandably negative: "This is going to go very badly for us when it gets out." Everyone in the meeting really wanted to avoid the pain associated with dealing with the problem. They were emotional and afraid. It prevented them from making good, balanced decisions. That's when rationalization crept in— the enemy of otherwise pretty good people. Someone in the room stated something that would result in little to no action. Someone else added something to the lame response to the known problem. It was hard for compliance professionals to help because the meeting was filled with people who wanted an easy out. The result? A poor decision based more on emotions than facts.

> **ROY'S RULE**
>
> Watch for rationalization and stop it before it infects leadership's decisions. Remember: It's the compliance professional's job to have honest conversations with leadership, whether or not advisors agree.

The truth is that these advisors will likely lead their organization down a path that looks a lot like a cover-up. People who have nothing to do with the original offense lose their jobs and the organization suffers a PR nightmare. The road is littered with these people.

FIGHTING RATIONALIZATION

The challenge is: *How do you fight rationalization?* To cut through the distraction of peoples' rationalizations, I always just laid key sentences from the regulation in front of them . . . right next to the evidence of what they were doing. I tried to make the problem as simple as possible to see. I let them rant and then came back to the two documents in front of them. I wouldn't fall down their rabbit hole of rationalization. If you do that, you will lose. Stay focused and have very specific evidence.

I also had honest conversations with leadership. I've always felt that telling leadership

> ## " I wouldn't fall down their rabbit hole of rationalization. "

the truth in a short, simple, and direct way is the best method out of a mess. I told the people in the room that organizations had taken the deny-and-defend approach so often that it caused society and the enforcement community to get tougher on them. I shared case studies of organizations that thought they did enough, but didn't . . . and the public later deemed their minimalist reaction to the problem was a cover-up. I said: "If you get this wrong, you are going to go from innocent to guilty overnight, and ironically you did not commit the offense that caused all this." I told them their personal risk would go from very high to very low, but only if they responded to the offense in a strong and measured manner. I tried to have all my conversations with the whole team when possible. But if I was getting buried by others who wanted to do nothing, I would have a private conversation with the top leader.

Let me be very clear: *leadership needs to understand that doing something in response to a known problem is good.* Society and the enforcement community will settle for no less than all-out war on major problems. Advisors want to be able to check the "I did something" box. *That's not how this works. That's not how any of this works. That's not enough.*

Following are some things you might say to leadership after the discovery of a problem. This is particularly helpful when others try to help leadership rationalize doing less than they should. Tell leadership that:

- The question is not how we check the box of having responded properly.

- The question is not how little we can do in response to this.
- The question is not how much the perp has done for anyone.
- This is no time to discuss your "risk appetite" with the risk manager.
- This is no time to calculate the odds of getting caught.
- This is not the time to mention, "Other organizations do this all the time."
- This is no time to discuss the odds of being able to defend the case with legal counsel.
- The question is not: *Who knew what when?*
- You found a problem and you have to have legitimate discipline and disclosure.
- The questions is: *What would an unbiased fair-minded person experienced in determining penalties do?*

When I speak about taking action, I'm not necessarily just talking about more discipline. Dole out as much discipline as you think is warranted. But remember, discipline is not the only reaction you can have to show people how seriously you take a major issue in your organization. In fact discipline is rarely ever visible (nor should it be). Instead, there are many relatively harmless visible actions you can do to prevent your reaction from looking like a cover-up. You can mandate more compliance education, change or update policies, and investigate other areas that might have the problem your organization is facing. That's what society and the enforcement community looks for in the end. Sure they want discipline and the problem to stop, but they really want to see action, contrition, and as much transparency as you can muster. Whatever you do, the net effect has to look like the leader stood at the top of the building and screamed, "I am mad as hell and I am not going to take it anymore."

I would also consider talking to others who advise leadership. I would talk to them about the problems rationalization causes and tell them some of the same things you tell leadership. They may not all help you convince leadership to respond to the problem properly, but you might be able to take the edge off their propensity to rationalize doing less. You could add a simple line or two to your leadership compliance training about the need to make sure reactions are appropriately strong enough for the problems that arise, long before leadership faces these sorts of decisions. I would consider working in a story or two about organizations that rationalized doing too little into random conversations with informal leaders. If you talk to people who will eventually be involved in disciplinary decisions throughout the course of the year, you can build a foundation of strength. I have watched effective compliance professionals educate leadership to the point that when tough decisions are made, the compliance professional doesn't have to say anything when rationalization rears its ugly head. Leadership already knows how to avoid it. And when that happens, *it's a beautiful thing.*

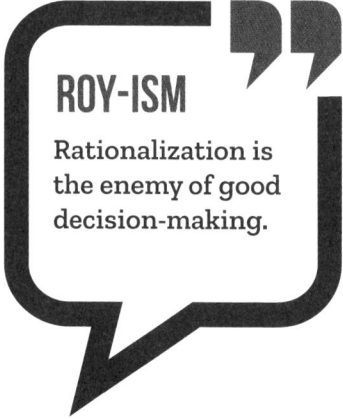

> **ROY-ISM**
>
> **Rationalization is the enemy of good decision-making.**

LESSON 13
VICTORIA AND
THE FALSIFIED LOGS

People never seem to know what compliance professionals actually do. It's very frustrating. They think we create the rules they have to follow, when in reality compliance professionals create the process of following rules others impose on them. They think compliance is all about punishment, when in reality compliance finds problems early so fewer people are punished.

Recently I visited Victoria, someone I've known for 10 years. I knew she worked in healthcare, but we never really talked about what I do. When I told her, she threw her head back and said, "*Nooooo, you're one of those Joint Commission guys!*"

No, I am not one of those Joint Commission guys. The Joint Commission is a credentialing body for healthcare organizations and programs. If you break their rules, your healthcare organization can't be certified by them. Certification makes these organizations and programs eligible to receive federally funded payments from The Centers for Medicare & Medicaid Services programs. It is voluntary, but many healthcare organizations view it as essential.

"We don't make up rules," I told her. "We help people follow the rules and have nothing to do with The Joint Commission. You are a perfect example of how people spread misinformation about compliance professionals."

It was obvious to me that Victoria's organization was missing an effective compliance program.

VICTORIA'S PROBLEM

She went on to say that it was impossible to comply with The Joint Commission's overbearing rules, something her organization wanted employees to do. She cited one rule in particular. It was aimed at people who work with child patients and have toys available for them to play with. The requirement is to wash the toys . . . a ridiculous number of times each day.

"So I falsify the toy-washing logs," she said.

That's when I said, "Your case study has just gone from good to priceless. I am going to write about you in my book!"

What Victoria did goes on everyday all over this country—*good people doing bad things*. She's bright and funny, and a very, very good person. She has a college education and an advanced degree. Plus, she's dedicated her life and career to helping children. Yet Victoria is totally lost on the risks associated with falsifying a toy-washing log at a healthcare organization.

She sees the toy-washing rule as being ridiculous and a waste of time. Instead of washing, she wants to spend all the time she can helping her patients. So she falsified the toy-washing log. Sadly, what she thinks and does makes sense to many people. A majority of the population would side with Victoria. They would side with her until it all went wrong. Then Victoria would be the scapegoat for a scandal resulting from her misconduct.

THE NIGHTMARE SCENARIO

Here's what could possibly happen from Victoria's misconduct. Let's say one sick kid came in and played with the toys. He had a particularly bad illness. Then another kid with other complicating health factors played with that toy, got sick, and died. After conducting an investigation, the compliance department discovered that Victoria falsified the toy-washing log. Lawyers have a field day debating who was at fault. Whatever conclusion they came to, I assure you that when the whole thing was over, Victoria's career would be over too . . . and some coworkers, friends, and family would consider her a pariah.

As I sat there explaining how Victoria could get into serious trouble, the look on her face was dripping with the look compliance professionals get all the time: *You compliance nerd, that will never happen*. It's not that it happens often; it's that it's devastating when it does. The data in this case is helpful: according to The Centers for Disease Control and Prevention, 1 in 31 US hospital patients contract a healthcare-associated infection each day.[1] People die from those healthcare-associated infections each year. This is a perfect example of why trained risk professionals factor in the severity of consequences when they determine risk. If something is rare, but has deadly consequences when it does happen . . . *it's high risk*! The people who ignored the slim chance of something happening and had that rare problem occur believe me, because their lives were ruined. Many who have not had that experience just write me off as a compliance nerd. They offend me and yet I feel badly for them, because they are at risk of having their lives ruined.

I have seen countless examples of good people finding ways to work around a regulation . . . and then they end up in monumental trouble. No one came to those people and told them stories about how good people ended up in serious trouble. No one investigated or audited Victoria's toy-washing logs. No one did compliance training in her department. No one then interviewed a couple people after to ask if they knew of anyone doing anything wrong to find problems. Victoria is the victim of a horse crap compliance program. She hates compliance and thinks compliance professionals make up rules. Ironically the people whose job she hates are the people who could help her find a pretty painless way to deal with her problem.

> ## ROY'S RULE
>
> Sometimes people only focus on the fact that there is a very slim chance of something happening. They don't think about factoring in the worst case scenario when calculating risk. We need to teach people a little about risk determination:
>
> - Slim chance of causing a problem + minor outcome = *low risk*
> - Slim chance of causing a problem + a seriously negative outcome (like death) = *high risk*

HOW COMPLIANCE HELPS

What would I do if I was her compliance officer? I would say, "Show me the rule about toy-washing and take me to the toys." I would ask her to describe her day and her process. I would ask her to show me where she washed her toys. I would observe her practices and take notes.

Then I would make a couple calls to people with similar jobs in other organizations and see how they deal with toy-washing. I would search the internet for machines that automated the cleaning process. And I would take her through this whole process with me. I bet you 12 bucks that before I even had an alternative to her cheating, she would think of the solution herself. If she really understood the risk to herself and her peers, she might even write about her solution in her professional association's magazine and give speeches about it to people in her profession. Then other good people might avoid falsifying their toy-washing logs. And who do they owe it all to? That pin-headed nerd compliance professional—*me*. If all that happens and you write about it, please refer to me as the "Compliance Illuminati." *Thank you, thank you very much.*

As you do your job in the compliance department, remember to let employees know that compliance professionals are not regulators. We don't make up rules: we help people find a way to follow rules. We find problems early when they are small. To fight people's misperceptions, find ways to educate employees about compliance programs and the role of compliance professionals every chance you get. Put it in the introduction of every presentation. Hang up posters. If you have more training time, find one of the hundreds of stories like Victoria's. Share how a good person did something wrong and no one helped her before it all went south. Tell employees, "The person who could have helped was me!"

We have to do a better job educating people about compliance. And don't stop at just teaching the average employee. Insist on teaching this to leadership too. Insist on getting time with the board to explain what you do. Pull out case studies documented in the press about regular people getting

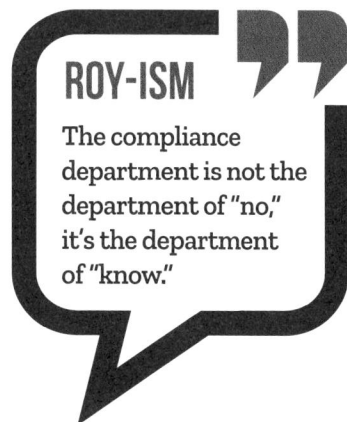

> **ROY-ISM**
>
> The compliance department is not the department of "no," it's the department of "know."

into horrible trouble. Above all, remember that as a compliance professional, you are a teacher. Although we do help provide our organization with audits, legal analysis, risk assessments, and more, our profession was created to build awareness about compliance and ethics amongst our otherwise very bright colleagues.

LESSON 14
THE POSSIBILITY OF BEING TOO ETHICAL

In 2014, former FBI Director James B. Comey gave the keynote speech at our Compliance & Ethics Institute in Chicago. When introducing him, I said that I believed the FBI had one of the best compliance programs of any government agency. Comey thought so too, stating that the FBI was very proud of their compliance program.

Comey went on to speak about cybersecurity, and how to deal with cyber threats. He said that these threats don't always come from outside a company, they often come from inside—contractors, employees, system administrators—people with a grudge or some problem with someone or something in the company. Comey also spoke about the importance of building a culture where people care about one another and the security of the company. If this kind of culture exists, then employees feel safe sharing anything they notice that could harm the business.

That was the second time I had met Comey. On both occasions he was very impressive. However, shortly after this presentation, all heck broke loose at the FBI. Here's a little recap of what happened, and how Comey broke with FBI policy in 2016 in regard to the investigation of Hillary Clinton's use of private servers and email system for government work while secretary of state.

COMEY'S DECISIONS

On July 5, 2016, while the investigation was still ongoing, Comey called a press conference to give a public update on the FBI's findings so far. The Department of Justice (DOJ) has a policy that: "Any communication by DOJ personnel with a member of the media relating to a pending investigation or case must be approved in advance by the appropriate United States Attorney or Assistant Attorney General, except in emergency circumstances," and that the "DOJ generally will not confirm the existence of or otherwise comment about ongoing investigations."[1]

Yet, Comey broke these policies for this particular case. He noted in his press conference that his update was unusual in a few ways, saying: "First, I am going to include more detail about our process than I ordinarily would, because I think the American people deserve those details in a case of intense public interest. And second, I have not coordinated this statement or reviewed it in any way with the Department of Justice or any other part of the government. They do not know what I am about to say."[2] Comey did not consult with Attorney General Loretta Lynch or Deputy Attorney General Sally Yates about the public announcement. I am not entirely sure of the reason why he did not consult with them, other than some speculation about a conflict of interest created by a meeting between the attorney general and the subject of the investigation's husband, former President Bill Clinton.

During the press conference, Comey stated that the FBI did not find evidence that Clinton intended to violate laws about the handling of classified information, but rather found that she and her colleagues were extremely careless in how they handled the emails.

A few months later, on October 28, Comey sent a letter to Congress stating that more of Clinton's emails had been found while investigating another case. He stated that the FBI was going to investigate these emails. Then on November 6, Comey sent another letter to Congress stating that after reviewing the additional emails, there were no changes to the FBI's conclusions.

THE DOJ'S COMPLIANCE REPORT

At the request of Congress, Inspector General Michael E. Horowitz announced the DOJ would investigate Comey's actions and possible misconduct regarding the investigation of Clinton's emails. Horowitz is basically the compliance officer for the DOJ. He's also someone I know well, as he is a former SCCE advisory board member. Horowitz is better at unbiased investigations than anyone I have ever met. I desperately don't want to get into the politics related to the trouble Comey got into as director of the FBI; instead I'll refer to Horowitz's report about the compliance issues at question.

In part, the main compliance question was: *should Comey have shared information about an ongoing FBI investigation with the public?* In June 2018, the Office of the Inspector General issued its findings. The summary of the report stated that:

> We determined that Comey's decision to make this statement was the result of his belief that only he had the ability to credibly and authoritatively convey the rationale for the decision to not seek charges against Clinton, and that he needed to hold the press conference to protect the FBI and the Department from the extraordinary harm that he believed would have resulted had he failed to do so. While we found no

evidence that Comey's statement was the result of bias or an effort to influence the election, we did not find his justifications for issuing the statement to be reasonable or persuasive.

We concluded that Comey's unilateral announcement was inconsistent with Department policy and violated long-standing Department practice and protocol by, among other things, criticizing Clinton's uncharged conduct. We also found that Comey usurped the authority of the Attorney General, and inadequately and incompletely described the legal position of Department prosecutors.[3]

It went on to state that although Comey "'believe[d] very strongly that [the FBI's] rule should be, we don't comment on pending investigations' and that it was a 'very important norm' for the Department to avoid taking actions that could impact an imminent election, he felt he had an obligation to update Congress [on October 28] because the email discovery was potentially very significant and it made his prior testimony no longer true."[4]

 The DOJ "found that in making this decision, Comey engaged in ad hoc decisionmaking based on his personal views even if it meant rejecting longstanding Department policy or practice . . . [and that his] description of his choice as being between 'two doors,' one labeled 'speak' and one labeled 'conceal,' was a false dichotomy. The two doors were actually labeled 'follow policy/practice' and 'depart from policy/practice.' Although we acknowledge that Comey faced a difficult situation with unattractive choices, in proceeding as he did, we concluded that Comey made a serious error of judgment."[5]

EXTREME INTEGRITY

I want to just focus on one aspect of this: *What was Comey's overarching reason for breaking a long-standing DOJ policy that he supported?* As Horowitz said in his report, Comey decided that he was faced with an ethical dilemma of choosing between two doors: one labeled "conceal" and the other labeled "speak." Horowitz thought this was a false choice: Comey actually chose between following policy or not. Comey as much tells us that ethics drove him to define the two doors in the way he did. So did ethics cause this problem?

I think this is what happens when people overreach ethically. It's kind of like we can't see straight when we become hyper-ethical. Comey even named his book: *A Higher Loyalty.* The higher loyalty he is referring to is ethical leadership. The irony here is he broke long-standing rules of the organization where he worked in the name of being an ethical leader.

I believe Comey is a man of very high integrity, and that the pressure of the situation caused his integrity to escalate to a point that was beyond helpful. I believe Comey felt that the situation called for extreme integrity, and he felt that he had so much integrity that he could break policy. Comey felt that he and only he could get this right. Is it possible he had too much integrity? Sounds ridiculous, but personally, I think it's entirely possible. My concern is that it could happen to any of us. I bring this all up to say that we must be conscious of this risk.

> ## ROY'S RULE
>
> Beware of becoming "hyper-ethical." Anything taken to its extreme can become problematic.

Did Comey make a mistake? I will let you be the judge of that. Is it possible to think you are so ethical that it justifies breaking company policies? Is that right to do so? I have had compliance professionals call me up ranting about their terrible, unethical companies. They talked endlessly about their company's mistakes and essentially told me that they should decide every ethical question the organization asks. Everyone else's views didn't matter. No one was going to influence their decisions. They would not consult anyone—and anyone who disagreed with them was unethical. They were the epitome of self-righteousness based on ethics.

We all run the risk of rationalizing our policy-breaking actions with our ethical principles. It may not be too often, but I think it does happen. As is the case with many things, there is a spectrum of ethical reactions to a problem—going from unethical to just about right to too ethical. Anything in excess can be troublesome. I just think that as compliance professionals we have to be careful of this, because being too ethical is almost a job hazard.

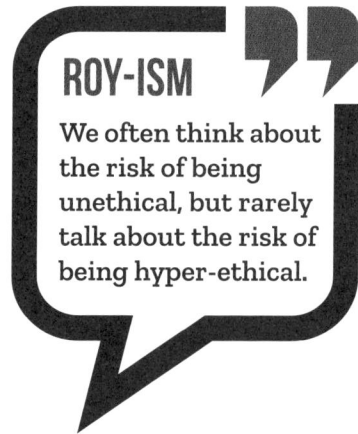

> **ROY-ISM**
>
> **We often think about the risk of being unethical, but rarely talk about the risk of being hyper-ethical.**

LESSON 15
A GUIDE TO BEING DELIGHTFULLY HONEST

We were at a leadership meeting and the discussion had been a particularly tough one. For an hour or so, everyone was stressed while we worked out a plan to fix our issue. At the end of that meeting, I could see how drained everyone was. I had taken a very strong stand and was pretty passionate throughout the discussion. So, I said, "Other than that . . . I feel pretty neutral about the whole thing." Then everyone laughed as we got up to leave.

When I walked out of the meeting with my CEO, he turned to me and said, "I really appreciate how you use humor in our leadership meetings." I was lost (as I often was with my greatest mentor Marc Dettmann)—he was always a few steps ahead of me. Marc went on to say, "You pick the right moment to make everyone laugh and lighten the mood. After a difficult conversation, you say something funny, people relax, and then we all move on. It reduces the tension."

I was unaware of what I was doing, but it all made sense when he explained it to me. I think the reason why I started doing that was to make people feel better. I often waited until the difficult conversation was over (rather than while it was happening) so my humor would not appear to be making light of anyone's perspective or downplaying the issues discussed. Years later, I realized that I was promoting honest conversation. My jokes helped reduce the pain that can come from having an honest conversation. Telling those jokes inadvertently promoted the honest conversations this CEO wanted to have.

Honest conversations can be painful, especially when everyone in the room is dealing with a tough choice. We all are reluctant to be honest. We all contribute to the problem. By trying to be funny at just the right moment, I was telling everyone: *It's okay. We're all good, so let's move on.*

BE HONEST, GAIN TRUST

Wanting to be honest is one thing—making it happen on a regular basis is a whole different thing. Honesty is not as simple as it sounds. Yet, as a compliance professional, you ask everyone around you to be honest. But before they can be honest with you, they need to trust you. How do you gain their trust? By also being honest with them. Trust and honesty are two very important tools in a compliance professional's toolbox. Compliance professionals often ask people to do difficult things. Your success in convincing people to take a particular action is based in large part by how much trust they have in you.

So what does it mean to be honest? Whenever I write about this subject, I get emails from people thanking me and basically saying, "I'm told I'm a jerk and I say that I'm just being honest. Thanks for encouraging and supporting me." But what I want to tell them is: *Don't thank me. I don't support people who are jerks hiding behind a cloak of honesty.* Not all honesty is the same—it can be rude or whiny . . . to good . . . to delightfully honest. I'm supportive of people who are *delightfully honest*— with unfiltered, unaffected honesty delivered with a smile that comes across without offending anyone.

I just met someone who is delightfully honest. Her name is Beverly Kracher, and she runs the Business Ethics Alliance in Omaha, Nebraska. Sometimes I get this feeling that I am missing something and it haunts me. It really bugs me when the feeling I have is that I'm missing something good. This happened after a few email exchanges with Beverly. It was pretty funny, actually. After the first email, I tilted my head to the side like one of those funny dog videos, but I had no idea why. Then one more email came, then another, and then I got it—she was being delightfully honest. In our email exchange, I made some observations about her success and perspective, and that I thought they were unique and effective. She shared something about how people view her unique approach and how some people don't really get her or agree with her. And she did so without throwing those who disagree with her under the bus. She was matter of fact about it, not defensive. She shared her thoughts on a sensitive topic as if she were commenting about the taste of a particular tea she was sipping. There are many people like Beverly in the compliance profession. Our profession attracts delightfully honest people and nurtures their honesty.

> **ROY-ISM**
>
> Honesty is the best policy, but delightful honesty is the best strategy.

15 TIPS FOR HONEST CONVERSATIONS

1. Talk about important truths with the same disposition as ordering a cheeseburger.

2. Often smile as you speak and remain delightful when others don't.

3. Ask questions after sharing something significant.

4. Don't criticize others' truth or try to jam yours down their throat.

5. Get to the point quickly and don't feel a need to talk all the time.

6. Don't interrupt.

7. Read people well and know how far to push an issue.

8. Study how people in the discussion are doing.

9. Disagree in an agreeable way and ask questions to help others see what they are missing.

10. Listen, see what others are not seeing, and share.

11. Nod while talking, not necessarily in agreement, but instead to encourage others to talk.

12. Love the process of sharing truths with others more than you want to change them.

13. Don't argue; have a conversation.

14. Look for the proper time to jump in and let others share their truths first.

15. Use humor, typically self-deprecating humor, to let everyone know everything is okay after a tough conversation.

WHAT MAKES SOMEONE DELIGHTFULLY HONEST?

I have met people who are honest, but something seems to be missing. Some honest people seem more honest than others, and I don't mean in the obvious way. The question for me is: *Why am I more impressed by or interested in some honest people over other ones?* Being delightfully honest is not just about telling the truth: actions, reactions, engagement levels, and conversational skills are all wrapped up in honesty too. Technically, you can tell the truth, but leave some truth out. Not being in the moment can cause you to miss what the other person is saying or thinking. Bias, lack of knowledge, limited common sense, and much more all play a role in an honest conversation. Over the years, I've noticed that many honest people share some of the same traits. When I find a person with all of these traits in alignment, it's a rush for me. There is some joy to finding someone who can do this well. Here are some of the best traits and actions of the delightfully honest people I've encountered:

Open and Seek Deeper Truths

I know plenty of people who are honest, but they're also very guarded. They really don't share everything they think about a subject. It's not inappropriate—they are still honest, but something is missing. I really like to get to a deeper truth, and openness is a way to get there. Open people are more interestingly honest. I try to be open first, which sometimes helps other people be open too.

Take Risks and Don't Freak Out

Delightfully honest people take conversational risks. Then they don't freak out if what they say is correctly rebutted by someone else. They explore uncharted territory and encourage others to take conversational risks too. These honest people artfully correct others when they are wrong, or just let it go. You can help people take risks just by being easier on them.

Situational Awareness

I once asked my father what he thought about my boss. He said, "He has his feelers out. He is constantly looking for information about how you feel about something and what you think." When that boss talked, he talked about everything related to what we were being honest about, because he was in the moment. He wasn't just concerned about *his truth*. He kept the conversation on the truth relevant to both parties.

I suggest you pick a few conversations in the near future and do your best to stop thinking about what you are going to say next. Try thinking only about what the other person is saying, thinking, and trying to say. If you want to take it a step further, try to help that person explore the truth and get the point across. Do this for an uncomfortably long period of time. It may seem strange, but explore their truth and then share your perspective. It can be awkward, but sometimes you learn more about a soft skill like this if you go all in. Then later you can do this more naturally.

Use Common Sense

Common sense, it seems to me, helps you go to much deeper and more interesting places in an honest conversation. Know that there are many different kinds of common sense—social, political, business, management, family, skilled trades, and more. I encourage you to steer your conversations to people's strengths, rather than their weaknesses.

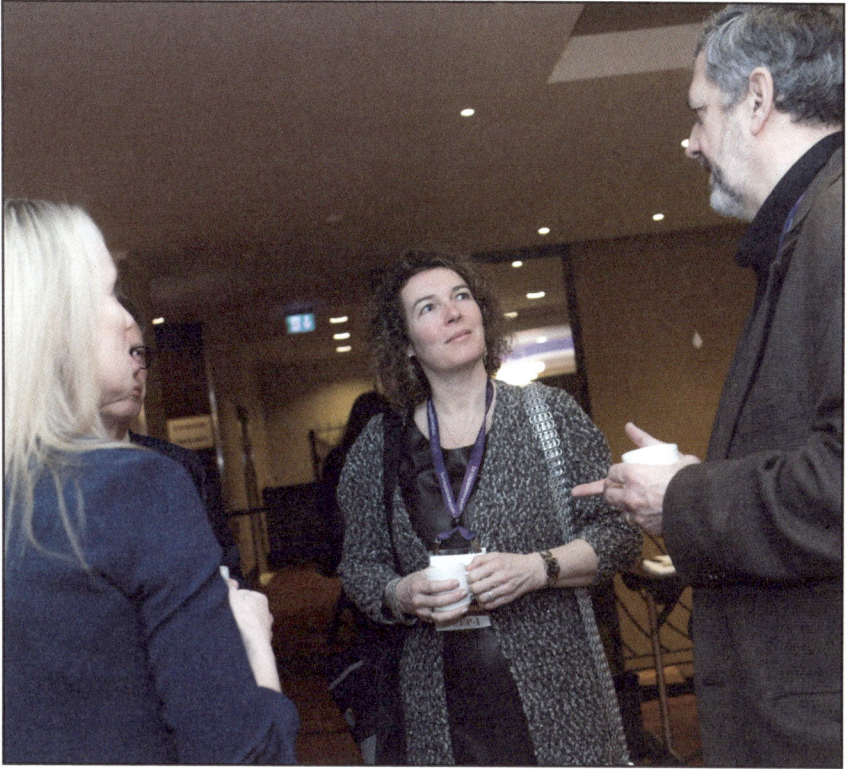

You are who you hang around with all day and I am a better person for hanging around compliance professionals.

Keep the Conversation on Track

Pay attention to where you want the conversation to go. Delightfully honest people consciously try to figure out and remember the overarching topic you both are exploring. Then they keep the conversation on track. If you wander off-topic, they bring you back to where the conversation was going before. They might say: "Tell me more about what you said a minute ago. What did you mean by that?"

Self-Awareness

Pull back when being honest about an unfamiliar subject and acknowledge that you don't understand it very well. That shows your honesty. I am impressed by people who know their limits on a particular subject or acknowledge when they are rendering an opinion.

Encourage Others and Enable Truth

Help people discover the truth on their own, rather than just hitting them over the head with it. I get pretty wound up and too direct in some discussions, and it rarely helps. You will be more effective if you take your time and ask questions that help people put two and two together properly. Here's an example. I had lunch with someone who was delightfully honest. He was talking about a subject that I really didn't understand or necessarily agree with. Rather than disagree, I tried to encourage him to explore his truth more. I didn't derail his journey with my version of the truth.

I struggle with trying to correct people when I think they are wrong. I often even start trying to correct them, only to find out that I didn't listen or understand their point and we were actually in agreement. I spend more time now trying to engage in a conversation to help someone else make their point (even if I disagree with it). The benefits are pretty significant—I feel better about myself, I learn, and I'm less stressed. I also get good ideas I can use later. When you find yourself desperately trying to take back the conversation to explain why someone is wrong, do just the opposite and help that person state his or her perspective more clearly.

Present All the Facts

Sometimes people are honest, but pull three out of 25 relevant facts to make a point. And the 22 other relevant facts don't support what they are saying. If you don't acknowledge all the available facts when making a point, you are technically being honest about three facts, but dishonest about the overall picture. This problem plagues our society. Really honest people will state all the pros and cons and then make their point known.

Put Bias Aside

People who want to have honest conversations put their bias aside for a while. Bias can lead to aggression, which can build up resistance to open conversation. People who can put their bias aside can have more truthful and honest conversations.

Keep Defensiveness Out

Have little-to-no defensiveness in a conversation. Smart people who want to deeply explore the truth consciously avoid saying things that put people on the defensive. There is a litany of defensive things not to say. Try asking questions that help others make their point. If you honestly try to help them, it's hard to offend them. I like to recognize things that trigger my bad behavior. Then I use that trigger to trigger better behavior. For instance, I get frustrated just before I become defensive. Someone says something and it triggers aggression. This leads to defensive statements or even just a defensive look. I try very hard to say to myself, *Roy, you feel offended*, and, *Danger, danger, you are going down the wrong path . . . ask a question, any question, ask anything to stall for time*. Simply saying, "Tell me more," can help. If nothing else, it buys you time. The longer you have to think before you talk, the greater chance you have of not being defensive.

Stay Curious

Honest conversations can be more interesting if you're talking with someone who's curious. I enjoy conversations with people who ask a lot of questions. They want to learn. Become more curious.

Seek Truth Uncompetitively

People who like to have honest conversations will not be competitive. Some people say things that come off as competitive and, like plaque building up in a hardening artery, it can block honest conversation. Those who are not out to "win" a conversation, allow others to comfortably explore their truths.

Keep Political Correctness at Bay

Being politically correct used to mean that you didn't call people disparaging names or engage in a few other serious indiscretions. Now being PC means not sharing opinions that someone else finds disagreeable. Out-of-control political correctness might be one of the biggest roadblocks to honest conversations our culture has ever experienced.

Let Go of What You Need

As I get closer to retirement, I find myself becoming more honest and open about my views. When I needed someone else's money, I was more careful about sharing my perspective. I also wanted acceptance, so I was more careful with my words. It is much easier to be completely honest if you don't need stuff from other people. Let go of what you might need or get from someone. It helps your honesty come through.

Cultivate Confidence

Confident people don't care who's right in a conversation. They just describe things the way they see them and listen to your perspective. Try to help people feel more confident, and you might get more interesting information from them.

Know that 1+1=3

Two delightfully honest people can advance the truth. One person says something that is true and interesting, and that triggers a related and interesting truth known by the second party. Then for a moment or two, both people have these two truths rolling around in their minds. Occasionally, one of the two people will say: "If both those things are true, then the following must be true." They never would have come to that unknown truth without that deep, open, and uncompetitive conversation.

Just Be Nice

Some people use honesty as an excuse for their bad behavior. Some people get in other people's faces a lot. They criticize and complain often. Their excuse for their bad behavior is that they are just being honest, when actually they are just being rude. Nagging, complaining, or being critical or mean is not honesty. It's bad behavior under the guise of being honest. Being nice is a core value of delightfully honest people.

LEARNING FROM THE DELIGHTFULLY HONEST

If you want to become delightfully honest, study those who do it well. Then start adopting some of their techniques. Interestingly, you have to study what delightfully honest people *don't do* as much as what they *do*.
I will leave you with some things that I have observed from the delightfully honest.

The person in my life who is remarkably good at this is one of my most important mentors: Dan Roach. He is the Cool Hand Luke of honesty. He learned a lot from his father Gene. I pay attention to how Dan shares his truth as

> **ROY'S RULE**
>
> When I find myself in a tense conversation where honesty and civility are necessary and hard, I imagine that I have my arm around the individual's shoulder as I tell that person what I need to say.

HONESTY FILTERS TO AVOID

I have no doubt that people who share their honest thoughts and views hope to be trusted. *There are so many good people*. But given what I've seen, some people filter their honesty. They filter it so they can:

- Tell people what they want to hear
- Get something they need from someone else
- Avoid offending others
- Prevent bullying from the "thought police"
- Appease the politically correct crowd
- Avoid criticism
- Impress powerful people
- Get someone to like them

These filters are like viruses that infect and degrade honesty. They may even impact some folks' definition of honesty. You have a right to filter your truth. But sorry folks, you do not have the right to filter truth and call it the "honest truth." *Filtered truth is an oxymoron.*

much as what truth he is sharing. You should consider doing this—*watch others share their truth*.

Find people who are wildly respected by their peers—someone who seems to get along with many people and gets invited to every meeting because others want this person's help. This someone makes people feel comfortable when having tough conversations. After you find someone to learn from, study *how* that person says things as much as *what* they say. Don't just watch when the person is speaking. Watch when that person is silent too. Watch that person watch the room.

Pay more attention to how people share their truths. Make a mental note of tricks they use to be delightfully honest. Start using those tricks too. Watch the things they do that put people off. Avoid doing those things yourself. Work on it for many years. You will make slow, incremental progress. You'll discover that the more delightfully honest you get, the less stressful and more informative your conversations will be.

LESSON 16
FIGHTING GROUPTHINK WITH DIVERSITY

At the 2018 CEI, I gave my goodbye speech to the members of one of the associations I helped build. I was so lucky to have this opportunity to be a cofounder and CEO. However, having to say goodbye was a bit much. It was a surreal moment. What I did to get past the emotion of the moment was to focus on the bigger picture. So I crafted an important message that I could send to those in attendance about the profession and our organization. I wanted to thank everyone involved, but especially paid tribute to the diversity of our board, organization, and profession as a whole.

"The entire organization and all of its accomplishments have been made by women and men," I said. "We haven't just checked the box of involving women in this organization, which many boards are still struggling to do. We have taken it a step further and taken advantage of all of the intelligence of the entire population, not just those with a deeper voice. It has been a huge advantage to us."[1]

Diversity strengthens any organization. At SCCE and HCCA, women are equally responsible for why we are where we are. Women haven't just been on our board, they have played key roles on our board. In the last 20 years, eight of our presidents have been women, including our current president Lori Strauss. My right-hand man for the past 15 years is not a man—April Kiel is the most unknown accomplished person

My farewell speech at the 2018 Compliance & Ethics Institute

this organization has ever had. She perfects our conferences, certification, customer service, publications, and much more. Our current immediate past president, Margaret Hambleton, has and will continue to be the star of the CEO transition process and is one of the most incredible leaders we have ever had. Debbie Troklus, senior managing director at Ankura, is a cofounder of our organization and has chaired the Compliance Certification Board since its inception. Debbie and many others have created the most respected and prolific compliance credentials in the world.

And while our board leadership has it all going on, this country is still struggling to simply check the box of gender balance in governance, let alone fully utilize the diverse perspectives represented in our country's population. Yet SCCE and HCCA are diverse within our leadership, membership, and volunteer ranks. People from many countries are deeply involved in our organization too—close to 10% of SCCE membership and annual conferences attendance consists of people living outside the United States. I would love to say we have embraced diversity within our organization because it's the right thing to do, but we really did it because it has given us an enormous competitive advantage.

> ## ROY'S RULE
>
> **Take advantage of all the intelligence around you, not just the intelligence of people just like you.**

WALKING GETTYSBURG WITH ODELL

The man who introduced me at my goodbye speech was Odell Guyton, someone who is very important to me. Odell is a professional colleague—he's the managing director of Klink & Company and cofounder of SCCE—but he is also a dear friend. We have vacationed together. I have met his family. He has helped me professionally and been a mentor to me. He has helped our organization since the beginning and has kept me from making mistakes. He has also done the best job of celebrating our success. But most important, Odell has been at my side as my understanding of the value of diversity has grown.

During his introduction, Odell recalled a three-day leadership training we participated in at the site of the Battle of Gettysburg. He said, "We walked the battleground. We traced the leadership challenges of that day and that bloody three-day battle. We learned that it was an ambiguous order from General Lee to General Ewell to quote, 'Take that hill, if at all practicable,' was one of the reasons that the battle was lost to the South, because the general failed to take that hill."[2] He went on to talk about my part (along with many others) in

Odell Guyton, my friend and colleague, introducing me at the 2018 Compliance & Ethics Institute

HCCA's and SCCE's success: "You've taken that hill—mission accomplished. You will always be remembered for these accomplishments, promoting our profession, and more importantly for being our friend."[3]

Odell and I have become great friends over the years and I remember that leadership training well. It was a few months before his presidency of HCCA and SCCE. Much of the training was held on the battlefield. We walked from the edge of the woods on one side of an open field across the same path soldiers took to get their enemy on the other side. It did not go well for those soldiers in that bloody battle. This walk with Odell meant a lot to me and we learned a great deal about leadership that day. However, the experience was far more poignant to me than its lessons about leadership. Here I was walking with one of the most respected leaders in our profession and our incoming leader. We were two compliance guys—one Caucasian and the other African American—retracing a battle critical to one of our country's biggest conflicts over racial inequality. It was not that long ago that that would have been difficult, if not impossible. I'm thankful to be living in a country where those of us who want to embrace diversity are encouraged to do so.

Diversity strengthens our profession and our compliance assessments and investigations in numerous ways. I asked Odell for his thoughts on why this is true. He said, "One of the most valuable but often understated tools that a compliance professional should possess and develop throughout their career is an appreciation for the different dimensions of diversity, including culture, race, ethnicity, gender, sexual orientation, socio-economic status, age, physical abilities, religious beliefs, political beliefs, or other ideologies. Taking diversity into account is invaluable in making credibility assessments related to compliance escalations and conducting follow-up investigations. A diverse compliance team enhances the compliance functions' credibility when reaching across geographic borders, influencing policy creation and dealing with various management teams and coworkers. Having appreciation for the value of diversity will greatly enhance your professional competency and program effectiveness."[4] I completely agree with Odell—compliance programs and professionals are much better off because of our profession's diversity.

DIVERSITY FIGHTS GROUPTHINK

From the beginning, compliance has also been professionally diverse. Since our profession came out of nowhere, people from other professions filled the ranks of our compliance teams. Naturally, people came from related professions that could contribute to a successful compliance program: audit, legal, risk, investigations, ethics, and more. Collectively, compliance programs have experience from every discipline. This gives us a big advantage over many other professions. A compliance program essentially takes diverse tools and uses them in a seamless, orchestrated way.

When a compliance department is diverse in different ways, the many perspectives of its members lead to better decisions. As our profession has sought to define the compliance officer's role and the compliance program's function, we have sat side-by-side with a diverse group of professionals to do so. One big advantage of this is that it fights groupthink—it's out of the question when making decisions with a diverse group of people. Groupthink is one of the great enemies of ethical behavior. Groupthink causes teammates to discuss problems in a myopic way.

Embrace diversity on your compliance team. Find the different perspectives that will inform and enhance your decisions. Fill the room with people who have diverse experiences and opinions. The result will be honest, open conversation that will help you

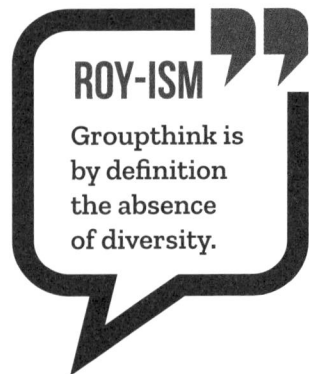

> **ROY-ISM**
>
> **Groupthink is by definition the absence of diversity.**

I feel fortunate to have been able to work with Odell Guyton, who has helped SCCE since its beginning.

make much better decisions. Bring in audit, legal, ethics, risk, investigations, and other departments as you implement your compliance program. Listen to them, they are experts in their field. See the diversity on your team and in your investigations as one of your biggest strengths. It will help you see the bigger picture of a compliance issue, better inform your decisions, and fight the decision decay resulting from groupthink.

LESSON 17
INDEPENDENCE: WHY IT'S CRITICAL

Accounting is a risk area. Marketing and sales is a risk area. Quality control is a risk area. That got me to wondering: *Aren't all departments risk areas?* If all departments are risk areas, should risk managers consider the legal department a risk area? In all my years in compliance, I have never heard anyone ask that question. Given that the compliance profession is so concerned about identifying risks, it seems that the question should have been asked by now and debated. The legal department makes the most complex and important legal decisions of any department in the organization. Some legal decisions also come with complex ethical ramifications that can magnify the risk. If not following the rule of law is a risk, should risk managers consider the department making most of the legal decisions a risk area?

So if legal is a risk area, why do some compliance professionals report to the legal department? And what are the conflicts of interest involved with that relationship? It's why I asked this question to a panel I facilitated for Corpedia in 2011: *What are the conflicts of interest that the enforcement community is concerned about when suggesting compliance officers be independent from legal departments?*

The panel's charge was to discuss current hot topics in the compliance and ethics profession. My question wasn't an easy one to answer for some of the panel members. One of them was Al Rosa, GE's chief compliance director and senior executive counsel. Rosa's answer was a bit of a long and winding road, and he never really answered the question. Instead, he answered a different question and then said he reported to the general counsel and supported that approach.

Ironically, I think that compliance officers who report to legal counsel might be too conflicted to answer the independence question. Interestingly, Rosa was not the only panelist who could not answer the question. So, I asked the audience. They came up with two reasons:

1. One person mentioned the compliance professional's annual review. Compliance professionals are frequently asked to investigate legal issues. Some of those issues are likely related to past legal decisions made by their boss—the general counsel.
2. Another person, the CEO of a compliance consulting company, added that the legal department is frequently asked to "circle the wagons and defend the company." She said the compliance officer should not be involved in circling the wagons, but rather provide an independent review of the problem for leadership.

This panel was quite typical. Those who want to report to the general counsel want to talk about its advantages, which typically are centered on the idea that the legal department and compliance department frequently work together to solve problems. People who want to report to the general counsel do not want to talk about the conflict of interest. A majority of compliance professionals consider the legal department their closest

> **ROY-ISM**
>
> **Independence is the most important element of a compliance program.**

partner. However, those that recognize the conflict of interest want to partner *and* have an independent reporting relationship.

ACKNOWLEDGE ALL CONFLICTS OF INTEREST AND RISK AREAS

Conflicts of interest are everywhere and compliance and ethics professionals should focus on them. They are at the root of many serious issues that go unresolved for years. The cure for conflicts of interest is independence. Our profession was created because society felt organizations needed an individual who is not conflicted to provide leadership with an independent assurance that ethical and legal problems are prevented if possible and found and fixed when not.

Conflict of interests were almost always at the root of significant legal and ethical issues that went unresolved over long periods of time. So at the core of our mission is to provide independent, unbiased advice to leadership so they can prevent, find, and fix their organization's ethical and regulatory problems.

> ## ROY'S RULE
>
> Conflicts of interest are at the root of almost all significant ethical and legal compliance issues that go unresolved for a long period of time.

There is risk every time we make an accounting decision. Similarly there is risk every time we make a legal decision. Therefore anyone, including the legal department, is a risk area. We should work hard with leadership to ensure our reporting relationship is independent. Staying independent will eliminate conflicts of interest and is key to making unbiased decisions and fixing problems. The compliance profession cannot help others manage their conflicts of interest if we have conflicts of interest too.

CORPORATE SPEAK

Some words are created to replace words that have become too negative. It's like companies that rename themselves after a huge PR disaster. Accounting fraud is sometimes referred to as aggressive accounting. People who think the term aggressive accounting has a bad connotation use the words creative accounting. Compliance officers who want to find problems early need to be aware of corporate speak and consider these words potential red flags for problems.

I once wrote an entire blog post consisting of corporate speak. I literally took two or three corporate speak phrases and put them together in a sentence randomly and the sentence kind of made sense. Then I wrote another corporate speak sentence and another to form a paragraph that kind of made sense. It's kind of amazing how much sense complete BS can make. Here's a whole paragraph of it:

> We will empower our employees to synergize our constituency. We will do the right thing by creating an ethical culture beginning with tone at the top to ensure our core values are aligned with our performance integrity standards. Ultimately we will mitigate the enterprise-wide risk assessment with our governance, risk and compliance plan. Our values-based performance Gant Chart will be mapped to our compliance program maturity model. Your leadership is providing this heads up as we gear up for the ramp up to the roll out. If you are an impactful team player, the ask will be to wrap your arms around the value proposition. And when we are done .... we will marinate the boilerplate with our risk appetite.

All I'm saying, is to be careful about valuing form over substance. That is another quote my mentor Marc loved to use when trying to get people to do good (rather than just look good). Some focus so hard on looking good, that they leave little time for getting anything done. Watch when departments start using corporate speak—it may be hiding a real compliance problem.

CONCLUSION

THANK *YOU* FOR YOUR SERVICE

Leaving SCCE and HCCA has made me think a lot about what these organizations have accomplished in the past 20 or so years. And one thought sticks in my mind—service. Our profession provides a great service to organizations of all kinds, your country, and the world.

I believe service is at the heart of compliance. It's one of many reasons why I wanted to include a tribute to another kind of service in our annual Compliance Institute (CI) conference—military service. I have always felt very strongly about those who risk their lives in service to our country. So, a few years ago we decided to have an auction for an organization that supports wounded veterans.

I sought out someone with a lot of experience to help us with the project—Kim Lansford, an exemplary compliance professional at Penn State Health and HCCA member whom I've known for years. Her son Justin is a retired army staff sergeant who was severely injured while on duty in Afghanistan in 2012. A roadside bomb exploded underneath the rear axle of his truck. As a result, Justin lost his left leg, crushed his right leg, broke his back, and suffered from many other injuries. Justin nearly died and was in the hospital and rehab for a very long time. When I called Kim and told her what we were up to for the conference, Justin had fully recovered and was helping other wounded veterans any way he could.

Justin tells his story and how America's Fund helped his family, along with Gabe (his service dog) and his mother Kim Lansford at the 2017 Compliance Institute

When I finished describing the project and suggested a charity we could contribute the proceeds to . . . there was a pause. After working with HCCA and SCCE members for all these years, I now know a pause is often what happens just before someone tells me a much better idea than my own.

I said, "Kim, is there a different organization that you prefer we work with?"

"Yes. All through Justin's ordeal, America's Fund helped us," she told me.

She explained how they had helped her family be with Justin during his hospital stay and all that they did to help him transition back to his life at home. It was very touching. So, I said, "Done deal."

We went on to raise a great deal of money for America's Fund. Ironically the organization I had suggested we raise money for went through a major scandal shortly after I called Kim. The CEO and COO were fired due to concerns about how the donated money was spent. An expert once again helped me dodge a bullet. I met and talked with Justin several times—*what a great human being*. He came to several of our conferences and brought his service dog Gabe, who stole the show. We've raised a great deal of money for America's Fund at CI conferences since 2014. We hope it shows how much we value our veterans' military service.

SERVING THROUGH COMPLIANCE

Many people have thanked Justin for his service at our conferences, and it got me thinking about our profession. Compliance professionals not only serve their organizations, but their work also serves their countries and, collectively, the world. Just think about how you and your work affects numerous people unknown to you—people in your organization, your city, your state, and beyond. The work you do is much bigger than you think. Thousands of compliance professionals working in the industry bring change that protects people's jobs, families, and society. It's not hard to imagine that . . .

> *Sometime in the next five years, one of you will prevent the next Enron scandal and people will not lose their pensions.*

HCCA and SCCE members are the people who will prevent the next corruption scandals from ever happening.

Sometime in the next year or two, some of you will discover people abusing others and stop them dead in their tracks . . . not years later.

Sometime this week, somewhere in the world, a few of you will find and stop someone from misappropriating someone else's money.

Sometime this week, some of you will stop an otherwise good person who is headed down the wrong path. You will stop the problem when it is small. The offender can be slapped on the wrist. The problem will not rot until the offender's career and life are ruined and family suffers.

Many people will not suffer because of you.

The work compliance professionals do helps people, and it also helps create trusted companies. Trusted companies create trusted countries. Trusted countries are successful in the global economy. Financially successful countries raise the standard of living for their people. Countries that are more ethical and compliant with the rule of law make citizens' lives safer, less corrupt, and just better. One compliance professional at a time has helped one organization at a time become a better place. Collectively, those companies have made their countries better places. Better countries make the world a better place too.

That is what your profession is all about. The compliance and ethics profession is a big damn deal and you are in the eye of the storm.

STEPPING DOWN

I recently stepped down as CEO of HCCA and SCCE. Because of my work as CEO and as a cofounder of these organizations, members thanked me profusely for my service to the profession. Quite often that is exactly what people said, "Thank you for your service," occasionally with tears in their eyes. It's caused me to reflect on my career and how I'll feel in my remaining years about what I've accomplished. There are two things that I want to take with me. With the help of many other wonderful people, we built something meaningful that will continue to help people long after we are gone . . . dare I say we built a legacy. Secondly, I would like to think that I provided a service to my country and helped the world become a better place through compliance. If this is even remotely true, I have you, our staff, and many other compliance professionals to thank for these accomplishments.

OUR NEW CEO: GERRY ZACK

Gerry quickly wins over the members he speaks with.

Replacing me as CEO of HCCA and SCCE is Gerry Zack. Gerry's had about five careers. He has spent a material amount of time in the audit, fraud investigation, risk management, accounting, and compliance professions. Something positive happens to you if you switch professions several times in your career. I am not sure about all of the effects of change, but I do know you become somewhat less biased. You are more aware of different skill sets and you appreciate the strengths and weaknesses of each profession. As committee members came out of their individual interviews with Gerry they shook their heads and all said, "He is going to be hard to beat." Gerry is honest, forthcoming, interesting, and interested. He is the kind of person you get to know quickly—it immediately feels like you've known him for a long time and he has a charming confidence about him. I think his professional experience is strong, but Gerry's interpersonal skills are stronger. It's why the SCCE and HCCA board unanimously selected Gerry.

Gerry and I worked together for a year—we were both essentially the CEOs of HCCA and SCCE for many months. We discussed problems and opportunities together, and I learned a lot about Gerry's temperament and leadership skills during that time. When a problem came up, he started asking questions. He stayed calm and never got frustrated, giving him a clear path to unemotionally gather facts. He has mad common sense too. After we gathered all the facts about a problem or opportunity, he would reach in and grab two or three of the most important facts, share them, and say, "Therefore I think we should . . . ." Few people I've met have his ability to determine the most relevant facts—a crucial skill for running an organization. He is open-minded, loves talking with people in the profession, and has an insatiable curiosity. You're going to love working with Gerry as he helps our profession get to where it needs to go.

I am the black silhouette in the back of this watercolor painting by my sister—she lovingly referred to me as the black sheep of the family.

What the members of HCCA and SCCE have done for me personally is profound. I have struggled my whole life to be a better person. I started out my life hanging out with the "wrong people," two of which ironically became lawyers. I don't think we were the "wrong people," but we did some things that resulted in my dear, sweet, loving sister calling me the black sheep of the family. She is a wonderful person and really meant it in a loving way.

Then around 23 years ago, I starting hanging out with compliance people. You are who you hang around with all day. I am a better person for having hung around you. For the last 23 years I have inched forward in the pursuit of being a better person and CEO. You have taught me to be more patient and look for the good in others. You have taught me to see people's strengths, not just their faults. You've taught me how to effectively influence others. You've taught me how to handle conflict and properly investigate problems before coming to a conclusion. You've taught me to respect the problems that often come with conflicts of interest. I've learned that the answer is not always to remove the conflict of interest, but rather to manage it. I've learned how to strengthen my emotional intelligence. I want to thank every board member who endured 30-minute calls from me, and who often talked me off a cliff or stopped me from making mistakes. *You are all my role models.*

I am too conflicted to assess what I have done, but I know what you have done—of that I have no doubt. I know for a fact you have served your country in your own way. From my accidental entry into the compliance profession to now, I've had the honor of working with some of the best people around. I have always tried to give more back to this profession than you have given me.

Thank you for this opportunity to serve as your CEO. Most of all, thank YOU for your service to me, this organization, and society. If you're looking, you'll be able to find me in my next office— either my shop or the remote Canadian woods . . . pretty far from most regulations.

AFTERWORD

I have been evolving. One of the things I have tried to do better is find people to work with who understand some important task. Then I let them do what it is they do. In other words: *I trust them*. I particularly like letting people who work in an often micromanaged profession . . . do their job. I get a kick out of telling them: "Cool, let's do what you said." I worked with Karen Latchana Kenney on something very important to me—this book, my first book. Karen is my editor. In the process of writing this book with her, I believe I have trusted her and gotten out of her way. I don't agree with everything Karen says, but I agree with damn near everything.

My writing has been evolving too. I've written a lot, but much of my writing is equivalent to a 100-yard sprint . . . mostly columns and blog posts. However, there is a huge difference writing 400 vs. 40,000 words. It's like I'm a sprinter running a marathon for the very first time. I do not know a dangling modifier from a mortified participle. And I once tried to spell the word "any" with two n's. It took me way too long to figure out what was wrong. What I'm trying to say is that writing this book has been a whole new ballgame for me.

I write like I speak, and I speak directly. This can make people feel uncomfortable. I am not a careful writer and a few colleagues have even said I was a bomb thrower who didn't have a filter. God knows what people who think I'm a toad say! Bomb thrower? No filter? Uncomfortable? *I call it the truth.* And I cannot write any other way, because I think it lacks integrity. Lacking integrity is a deal-breaker for me. So the only thing I asked Karen to do was to "keep my voice." I trusted her to do so. Trusting others is a risk. Speaking frankly is a risk.

To misquote Mike Tyson: *Everyone talks about how great it is to take risks until risk punches them back in the face.* To get something really good though, *you need to take a few risks.*

> **Everyone talks about how great it is to take risks until risk punches them back in the face.**

Most everything I write has a beginning, middle, and end . . . just not necessarily in that order. Karen told me that she looks for the "beginning" in my writing, and then I guess . . . she puts it in the beginning. After writing lesson after lesson for close to three months, I read through the entire book in one setting, as Karen told me to do, and made one last round of light editing. It was the first time I read what she "did to MY book." During the editorial process, I didn't read every lesson she edited—I skipped to the parts she wanted me to fix. She was a little nervous about whether or not I would like what she had done. I asked why and she said, "Because you hadn't read it as we went along in the process, and you might not like it." I don't trust blindly, but I do trust, and I admit it would've sucked if I didn't like what she had done. But Karen has written many books and edited many more . . . plus YoGI, who knows his stuff, picked her for this job.

After my first run through the whole book, I told Karen that I loved it . . . but that I thought the beginning was too long and maybe off point. She smiled that kind of smile you get when someone is glad you just figured out you were wrong, but they don't want to be overt about it. After we talked, I wrote something short and completely different, sent it to her, and said, "Do your thing."

Later, she came into my office to discuss the new introduction. She talked about what she was going to keep from the original and seemed pretty excited. Do you have any idea what happens when you delegate work and trust the right person? Do you have any idea how it makes them feel? Do you have any idea how much more effective trusted people are when they are allowed to be creative and do their thing with just a little guidance? You probably do understand, because it happened to you once . . . but not enough. So why don't you trust others as much as you want to be trusted?

Trusting people is a big damn deal to the person who is trusted, but, frankly, I delegate and trust because the work comes out faster and better. The return on the investment of your time and money is better when you trust rather than micromanage. The fact that people who are trusted are happier is just icing on the cake for me. What's most important to me is getting more crap done than the next guy, getting it done well, and doing all that on a timely basis. Trusting the right person does that.

Not only did Karen keep my voice, I could not for the life of me tell you what she changed—it was done so seamlessly. Karen actually interviewed people who knew me before we started. She wanted to figure out who I was and what I knew so she could pull it out of me and put it into this book. *Trust her? Are you kidding me?* She is the one who knows what is going on here. The concern should have been: *could she trust me to do my part?* I am the first-time book writer. It is one of the finest feelings I have experienced when working with others . . . effusive trust. She guided us to where we needed to go and the whole thing has been very cool. This isn't going to be MY book. This is going to be OUR book.

Effusive trust helped my first book get to where I wanted it to go. Effusive trust can also help a compliance and ethics program get to where you want it to go. You have a choice to make: do you want it to be "*your* compliance and ethics program" or "*our* compliance and ethics program?" If you choose to have it be *your* compliance and ethics program, I am pretty sure you will fail to improve. There is not enough time in the day to do it all by yourself, even with a well-staffed compliance department.

Every employee in the company has to own their compliance and ethics program. Everyone needs to be involved in education, implementing controls, listening to complaints, looking for problems, and more. Every department head needs skin in the game . . . or implementing a compliance and ethics program is going to be an uphill battle. Audit, legal, risk, communications, ethics, and many other departments are going to want to do part of "your job." If you are smart, you will let them do their part and *trust them*. Trust them as you would like to be trusted, but do keep an eye on them. If they don't do everything you need done, you will need to help fill in the blanks.

Have effusive trust and allow employees to own their company's compliance and ethics program. See what kind of compliance work you can accomplish together. Find people who can do the job that needs to be done, and then trust in them. I promise: *you cannot lose.* **RJS**

THE COMPLIANCE PROFESSIONAL'S
CREDO

This is a list of things I commit to as a compliance professional. It's not an exact science, an exhaustive list, or a standard—it's just my perspective. Use this credo as a starting point for your own compliance credo.

- I prevent, find, and fix ethical and regulatory problems and strengthen my organization's ethical culture using all elements of a compliance program.
- I am concerned about all risk areas and laws.
- I base my compliance program on Chapter 8 of the Federal Sentencing Guidelines.
- I regularly reread the Code of Professional Ethics for Compliance and Ethics Professionals to reset my focus.
- I am conflict-free, unbiased, and impartial.
- I seek support from my peers and I seek to support my peers
- Interpersonal skills such as collaboration, negotiation, and influence are keys to my success. I fully commit to having a strong emotional IQ.
- I help departments minimize the impact of compliance on business effectiveness.
- I help leadership effusively communicate their commitment to compliance and ethics.
- I regularly ask people throughout the company if they are aware of any problems. I don't just rely on the hotline. I make it easy for people to report issues.

- I regularly conduct compliance education sessions and then follow up with a few private interviews asking if employees are aware of any problems identified in the training.
- I protect those who report issues and facilitate trusted anonymous reporting.
- I use facts and the truth, and effect due process to protect those who are falsely accused.
- I will work with the organization's leadership to address known issues. I gather facts and tell leadership the truth. I'm not influenced by internal politics. I protect leadership from bad advisors and seek to keep all employees out of trouble. I report all material impediments to the implementation of an effective compliance program to leadership.
- I will report to a subcommittee of the board on a quarterly basis, the whole board annually, and regularly provide education to the board.
- I avoid finger-pointing and lecturing. I will recommend discipline when warranted.
- I consider risks created by partners, advisors, contractors, and third-party companies.
- I work *with* in-house and outside counsel—I don't work *for* them.
- I am aware that conflicts of interest create problems and can be the enemy of resolving problems. I seek to remove or effectively manage conflicts of interest when possible.
- I believe I need a seat at the table to prevent problems before they start.
- I will not participate in misconduct. Integrity is my core principle and I will not compromise it, even to right a wrong.
- I wait until a comprehensive investigation is completed before discussing specific details or recommendations, but will keep leadership generally aware of my progress.

- I only discuss possible ethical and regulatory issues with those who need to be involved.
- I am willing to delegate any compliance activity, but will assure it gets done correctly.
- I help everyone in the company take on some responsibility for compliance.
- I use outside specialists, not generalists, for high-risk activities.
- I cannot be responsible for both operations and compliance for the same area.
- If I discover an unrelated problem during an investigation, I will investigate it thoroughly.
- I do not let the pain from fixing a problem deter me and I will resolve it internally.

FURTHER READING

Here are some of the top books I recommend for learning more about compliance basics and the emotional intelligence needed for a career in this industry.

The Complete Compliance and Ethics Manual. **Minneapolis: Society of Corporate Compliance and Ethics, 2019.** Written by close to 100 authors, each experts on their subspecialty, this book covers the basics and more that every compliance and ethics professional should know.

Grant-Hart, Kristy. *How to Be a Wildly Effective Compliance Officer: Learn the Secrets of Influence, Motivation and Persuasion to become an In-Demand Business Asset.* **London: Brentham House Publishing Company, 2016.** If you are tired of compliance textbooks, buy this book. Grant-Hart gets into why interpersonal skills and influence are necessary to a compliance officer's success.

Murphy, Joseph E., and Joshua H. Leet. *Building a Career in Compliance and Ethics: Find Your Place in the Business World's Hottest New Field.* **Minneapolis: Society of Corporate Compliance and Ethics, 2007.** This book provides step-by-step instructions on how to start a career in compliance and ethics, describing the skills needed, the jobs available, how to find jobs, and other advice for people already working in compliance.

Murphy, Joseph E. *501 Ideas for Your Compliance and Ethics Program: Lessons from 30 Years of Practice.* Minneapolis: Society of Corporate Compliance and Ethics, 2008. This may be one of the most valuable books ever written for compliance professionals. It describes how to be successful, regardless of the size of your compliance budget.

Troklus, Debbie, and Sheryl Vacca. *Compliance 101.* 4th ed. Minneapolis: Health Care Compliance Association, 2016. This book of compliance basics is where to begin your journey in healthcare compliance.

Troklus, Debbie, and Sheryl Vacca. *Compliance 101.* 2nd ed. Minneapolis: Society of Corporate Compliance and Ethics, 2015. This book of compliance basics is where to begin your journey in compliance, regardless of your industry.

Troklus, Debbie, and Sheryl Vacca. *International Compliance 101.* 2nd ed. Minneapolis: Society of Corporate Compliance and Ethics, 2018. This book of compliance basics is where to begin your journey in compliance, regardless of where you live in the world.

Weiss, Art. *Building an Ethical Culture: Why It's Vital, How It's Done.* Minneapolis: Society of Corporate Compliance and Ethics, 2018. Want to learn how to build an ethical culture? This book tells you how using multiple strategies and techniques, and also explains why an ethical culture is so important.

SOURCE NOTES

INTRODUCTION

1. Fax memo to Roy J. Snell, "The Health Care Compliance Association: A New Forum for Health Care Professionals Involved in Compliance," January 22, 1997.

LESSON 3

1. Dan Roach, "Strategies for Enhancing Your Effectiveness as a Compliance & Ethics Officer" presentation at 2012 Compliance & Ethics Institute, October 15, 2012, video, 22:19-22:42. http://bit.ly/2S1ps7u.

LESSON 5

1. "Magnum Force Quotes," Quotes.net, STANDS4 LLC, 2018, accessed December 27, 2018, http://bit.ly/2GB0x8t.

LESSON 6

1. Jenny O'Brien, "Influencing Decision-Making session at the 2014 Compliance and Ethics Institute" presentation at the 2014 Compliance & Ethics Institute, August 25, 2016, YouTube, video, 46:53-47:22, http://bit.ly/2GCkHyW.

LESSON 10

1. Krista Lee-Jones, *U4 Expert Answer—Bosnia and Herzegovina: Overview of corruption and anti-corruption*, Transparency International, January 26, 2018, modified September 4, 2018, http://bit.ly/2GGHDxf.
2. Višnja Marilović, "The 13th Annual International Compliance & Ethics Award recipients: Bojan Bajić and Višnja Marilović" speech at 2017 Compliance & Ethics Institute, November 1, 2017, YouTube, video, 11:00-13:30, http://bit.ly/2BwQduP.
3. Višnja Marilović, "The 13th Annual International Compliance & Ethics Award recipients: Bojan Bajić and Višnja Marilović" speech at 2017 Compliance & Ethics Institute, November 1, 2017, YouTube, video, 11:00-13:30, http://bit.ly/2BwQduP.
4. Bojan Bajić, "The 13th Annual International Compliance & Ethics Award recipients: Bojan Bajić and Višnja Marilović" speech at 2017 Compliance & Ethics Institute, November 1, 2017, YouTube, video, 4:20-4:35, http://bit.ly/2BwQduP.
5. Bojan Bajić, "The 13th Annual International Compliance & Ethics Award recipients: Bojan Bajić and Višnja Marilović" speech at 2017 Compliance & Ethics Institute, November 1, 2017, YouTube, video, 5:30-5:35, http://bit.ly/2BwQduP.
6. Krista Lee-Jones, *U4 Expert Answer—Bosnia and Herzegovina: Overview of corruption and anti-corruption*, Transparency International, January 26, 2018, modified September 4, 2018, http://bit.ly/2GGHDxf.
7. Bojan Bajić, "The 13th Annual International Compliance & Ethics Award recipients: Bojan Bajić and Višnja Marilović" speech at 2017 Compliance & Ethics Institute, November 1, 2017, YouTube, video, 8:00-8:50, http://bit.ly/2BwQduP.
8. Višnja Marilović, "The 13th Annual International Compliance & Ethics Award recipients: Bojan Bajić and Višnja Marilović" speech at 2017 Compliance & Ethics Institute, November 1, 2017, YouTube, video, 15:06-15:26, http://bit.ly/2BwQduP.
9. Adam Turteltaub, "The 13th Annual International Compliance & Ethics Award recipients: Bojan Bajić and Višnja Marilović" speech at 2017 Compliance & Ethics Institute, November 1, 2017, YouTube, video, 0:00-1:59, http://bit.ly/2BwQduP.

10. Bojan Bajić, "The 13th Annual International Compliance & Ethics Award recipients: Bojan Bajić and Višnja Marilović" speech at 2017 Compliance & Ethics Institute, November 1, 2017, YouTube, video, 2:00-3:09, http://bit.ly/2BwQduP.
11. Bojan Bajić, Email message to author, November 13, 2018.
12. Bojan Bajić, Email message to author, November 27, 2018.
13. Jonathan Watts, "Operation Car Wash: Is this the biggest corruption scandal in history?," *The Guardian*, June 1, 2017, http://bit.ly/2teXknc.
14. Carolina Mandl, "Brazil's Petrobras to pay $853 million U.S. fine in Car Wash probe," *Reuters*, September 27, 2018, https://reut.rs/2UT2xwN.
15. Jonathan Watts, "Brazil erupts in protest: more than a million on the streets," *The Guardian*, June 21, 2013, http://bit.ly/2MXAARR.
16. Jonathan Watts, "Operation Car Wash: Is this the biggest corruption scandal in history?," *The Guardian*, June 1, 2017, http://bit.ly/2teXknc.

LESSON 11
1. David Jesse, "Engler changes MSU's compliance structure. Here's why experts are skeptical," *Detroit Free Press*, October 29, 2018, http://bit.ly/2RV2j6g.

LESSON 12
1. Ayn Rand. *Philosophy: Who Needs It* (Indianapolis: Bobbs-Merrill, 1982), 18.
2. Karen Horney. *Our Inner Conflicts* (New York: W. W. Norton, 1966), 135.

LESSON 13
1. The Centers for Disease Control and Prevention, *2016 National and State Healthcare-Associated Infections Progress Report*, accessed December 12, 2018, http://bit.ly/2thoOc3.

LESSON 14
1. Department of Justice, "1-7.000 - CONFIDENTIALITY AND MEDIA CONTACTS POLICY," *Justice Manual*, last modified April 2018, http://bit.ly/2SIH789 (section 1-7.400).
2. James Comey, "FBI Director James Comey FULL STATEMENT on Hillary Clinton Email Investigation (C-SPAN)," July 5, 2016, YouTube, video, 0:48-1:10, http://bit.ly/2GA8cUB.
3. Office of the Inspector General, *A Review of Various Actions by the Federal Bureau of Investigation and Department of Justice in Advance of the 2016 Election*, (Washington, DC: US Department of Justice, June 2018), vi.
4. Office of the Inspector General, *A Review of Various Actions by the Federal Bureau of Investigation and Department of Justice in Advance of the 2016 Election*, (Washington, DC: US Department of Justice, June 2018), x.
5. Office of the Inspector General, *A Review of Various Actions by the Federal Bureau of Investigation and Department of Justice in Advance of the 2016 Election*, (Washington, DC: US Department of Justice, June 2018), x.

LESSON 16
1. Roy J. Snell, "Opening Remarks and Awards Presentation" speech at the 2018 Compliance & Ethics Institute, October 22, 2018, video, 4:55-5:25, http://bit.ly/2NOPeHT.
2. Odell Guyton, "Opening Remarks and Awards Presentation" speech at the 2018 Compliance & Ethics Institute, October 22, 2018, video, 1:10-1:32, http://bit.ly/2NOPeHT.
3. Odell Guyton, "Opening Remarks and Awards Presentation" speech at the 2018 Compliance & Ethics Institute, October 22, 2018, video, 2:21-2:34, http://bit.ly/2NOPeHT.
4. Odell Guyton, Email message to editor, December 18, 2018.

PHOTO CREDITS

ABOUT THE AUTHOR

Roy J. Snell is a cofounder and the former CEO of the Society of Corporate Compliance and Ethics & Health Care Compliance Association. As a former administrator of the Mayo Clinic in Rochester, Minnesota, he worked in IT, the business office, and laboratories. He is the former compliance officer for the University of Wisconsin Medical Foundation and Hospital. Snell is a frequent speaker and writer on subjects related to the compliance profession. He is currently working for HCCA and SCCE as a strategic advisor to the CEO and writing several books. Snell has a master's degree in Health and Human Services Administration.

PRAISE FOR *THE ACCIDENTAL COMPLIANCE PROFESSIONAL*

Adam Turteltaub CHC, VP of Strategic Initiatives & International Programs at HCCA/SCCE: *"Roy Snell may have ended up in compliance accidentally, but it was the best kind of accident. Here he shares a lifetime's worth of wisdom and insights that can benefit anyone from a new compliance officer to the most experienced veteran."*

Ellen Hunt, Senior Vice President, Audit, Ethics & Compliance Officer at AARP: *"Chock-full of wisdom that I wish I had when I started my compliance journey. Thank you Roy for always being a mentor."*

Brian Back, Senior Partner at Hansen Back Recruiting: *"Roy's anecdotes are at times serious, at other times hilarious, and still others heartwarming and motivational, and finally even romantic. Like his grandfather before him, Roy truly is a wonderful storyteller."*

Andrijana Bergant, independent compliance advisor and President of EICE: *"With illuminating insights and a perfect dose of wittiness, lessons from this book will help you to sharpen the focus of what a compliance officer's job is: to 'find and fix compliance issues,' in Roy's own words."*

Paul Fiorelli, Professor of Legal Studies; Director, Cintas Institute for Business Ethics, Xavier University: *"Roy Snell created a legacy of compliance professionals who support their organizations, and each other, that will make us all better off. Thank you Roy!"*

Eric R. Feldman, Senior VP, Affiliated Monitors, Inc., and Former Federal Inspector General: *"Just like the man himself, Roy Snell's book is a down-to-earth, common sense compass for compliance officers to follow to achieve both personal and professional success."*

Kristy Grant-Hart, CEO of Spark Compliance: *"Compliance officers throughout the world will benefit from Roy's candid take on the profession. Reading this book is like having a conversation with a profoundly talented mentor to everyone in the compliance profession."*

Richard Bistrong, CEO, Front-Line Anti-Bribery LLC and former FCPA violator: *"Reading his book gave me a first-hand appreciation of how Roy embraces that errors and misjudgments, while often regrettable, can be forgivable and moments of learning for an entire organization, not just the person or team that misjudged a situation."*

Chris Cazer, CEO of Osprey Software: *"Roy's book should be compulsory reading for all compliance professionals."*

Ben DiPietro, Thought Leadership, LRN, and Former Wall Street Journal Reporter: *"Roy Snell offers an introspective, personal, and heartfelt reflection on his career and profession [and] insights to benefit everyone from the first-day-on-the-job newbie to the most battle-tested veteran."*

Jay Rosen, CCEP, Vice President, Affiliated Monitors, Inc.: *"From an era when the Compliance Officer was the 'Office of NO,' Roy aspired to create a home where compliance practitioners can feel nurtured, understood and be in the 'Know.'"*

Matt Kelly, editor and CEO at Radical Compliance: *"This book is a pleasure for compliance officers to read. Those new to the profession will find plenty of practical advice; battle-scarred veterans will find a book-length valentine to the profession Roy loves so dearly."*